Opus 87

Egon Eiermann
Haus Eiermann, Baden-Baden

Essay
Gerhard Kabierske

Photographien / Photographs
Horstheinz Neuendorff

Edition Axel Menges

Herausgeber / Editor: Axel Menges

Dieses Buch entstand in Zusammenarbeit mit dem saai, dem Archiv für Architektur und Ingenieurbau am Karlsruher Institut für Technologie (KIT).

This book was produced in collaboration with the saai, the Archive for Architecture and Engineering at the Karlsruhe Institute of Technology (KIT).

ISBN 978-3-932565-87-8

Druck und Bindearbeiten / Printing and binding: Graspo CZ, a. s., Zlín, Tschechische Republik / Czech Republic

Buchgestaltung / Book design: Axel Menges

Inhalt

Contents

Gerhard Kabierske

Einfach oder komplex? Das Haus Eiermann in Baden-Baden – ein Gesamtkunstwerk

Er wolle ein einfaches Haus für sich bauen, ein Gebäude, das, additiv gefügt, jedem Mitglied seiner Familie ein eigenes kleines Haus böte. Die Grundrisse sollten den funktionalen Abläufen des täglichen Lebens entsprechen, die Form stringent aus der Konstruktion entwickelt sein und selbst das kleinste Detail durchdacht und stimmig sich dem Gesamten einordnen, da »das Detail das eigentlich Noble in der Architektur« ausmache.[1]

Die klaren Leitbilder des Architekten Egon Eiermann, die er in seiner Lehre den Studenten an der Technischen Hochschule Karlsruhe eloquent und mit Charisma propagierte, sollten auch die Grundlage für den Entwurf seines eigenen Wohnhauses bilden. Mit der Losung »Wir sind keine Maler, wir sind keine Bildhauer, wir sind Architekten« versuchte er, ein spezifisches Selbstbewußtsein des vernunftgesteuerten und alle Belange beim Bauen klug zusammenführenden Architekten zu vermitteln, der sich gegen die Subjektivität des bildenden Künstlers abgrenzt.[2] Doch erklärt sich das Haus Eiermann in Baden-Baden als besonders demonstratives Objekt seines persönlichen Gestaltens tatsächlich einzig durch Funktionalität, Rationalität, Klarheit, Angemessenheit und Stimmigkeit bis in jedes Detail, durch jene Begriffe, mit denen der Architekt seine Bauten selbst immer wieder als Ergebnis logisch-architektonischen Denkens zu erklären suchte? Brigitte Eiermann, die ehemalige Schülerin und Frau des Architekten – selbst Architektin, Mitbauherrin und Mitbewohnerin – beschränkt sich in ihrer Beschreibung des gerade fertiggestellten Neubaus auf diese Sicht ihres Mannes. Da ist von der Disziplin der Grundrisse, von deren augenfälliger Ablesbarkeit an den Ansichten, von der Orientierung der Gebäude nach Himmelsrichtungen sowie vom »einfachen Gebilde« die Rede oder schlicht vom Zweck der Balkone vor den Fenstern für das Reinigen der großen Glasscheiben.[3] Doch schon bei der Publikation in der Bauzeitschrift *Architektur und Wohnform* schwingt 1963 im erklärenden Text, den ebenfalls Brigitte Eiermann beisteuerte, ein anderer Ton mit: Ihren Mann geradezu entschuldigend, stellt sie fest, daß es eben doch kein »ganz einfaches« Haus geworden sei, denn »dem glühenden Liebhaber der Architektur« sei es während der Planung »unterlaufen, daß ein höchst differenziertes und sehr kostbares Gebilde entstanden ist«.[4] Die schwer zu beschreibende und in gewisser Weise aus der Zeit gefallene Aura des Baues versucht sie sogar mit asiatischen Weisheiten des Laotse zu fassen: »Schwer und Leicht vollenden einander, Lang und Kurz gestalten einander, Hoch und Tief verkehren einander, Vorher und Nachher folgen einander«.[5] Poetisch soll damit in kontrastierend gegenübergestellter Begrifflichkeit das umschrieben werden, was nicht ausgedrückt werden kann.

Tatsächlich stellt sich der Bau auch dem heutigen Betrachter keineswegs als »einfach« dar. Bereits bei der Annäherung über die Hauptzufahrt der Straße »Krippenhof« könnte der Kontrast zu den nahezu gleichzeitig entstandenen benachbarten Siedlungshäusern und Bungalows nicht größer sein, genauso wie zu den kalten weißen Schachteln, die diese inzwischen ersetzen und vermeintlich »Bauhaus-Stil« sein wollen. Schon von weitem in der Flucht der Straße am Ende der Sackgasse auftauchend, fällt der Blick auf ein außergewöhnliches Haus. Form, Materialität und Farbe entsprechen nicht dem Gewohnten. Auf dem relativ weiten Vorplatz angekommen, der auch als öffentliche Wendemöglichkeit für Fahrzeuge dient, entfaltet sich eine räumlich komplexe Szenerie, die Bühnenbildqualitäten besitzt: ein Wohnhaus aus zwei getrennten Baukörpern, im rechten Winkel zueinander stehend, mit Mauern und Terrassen eng miteinander verklammert, »Haus und Nebenhaus«, so die von Eiermann und seiner Frau immer wieder verwendete Bezeichnung von absichtlich nüchterner Bescheidenheit.[6] Links erhebt sich erhöht das große Haupthaus giebelständig zum Betrachter und fluchtet weit in die Tiefe. Vorne quer stellt sich einem traufständig das kleinere Haus in den Weg, wie ein Torhaus, das ein herrschaftliches Anwesen gegen die Öffentlichkeit abschirmt. Doch statt in einen Hof geht es durch die große Einfahrt im Erdgeschoß in eine halboffene Doppelgarage. Erst auf den zweiten Blick fallen die großen Terrainunterschiede auf. Das Gelände steigt nach links und nach hinten stark an, wobei die natürliche Topographie durch Menschenhand vollständig verändert wurde. Alles hier ist terrassiert, was den hineingruppierten Baulichkeiten aus Substruktionen und daraus herauswachsenden Baukörpern Monumentalität verleiht. Der Vorplatz ist auf ein ebenes Niveau abgegraben, eine gewaltige efeuüberwucherte Bruchsteinwand aus lokalem Buntsandstein, der einzige Rest des alten Krippenhofs, fängt den Hang ab. Wie ein »Repoussoir« auf alten Gemälden schafft die Mauer im Vordergrund als eine von der Seite herangeschobene Kulisse räumliche Tiefe. Daß das große Haus in gleicher Richtung fluchtet, verstärkt den Zug in die Tiefe. Rechts im Bild, auf der Talseite, wird die Szene von einer niedrigen Mauer begrenzt, die, hakenförmig abgewinkelt, die Verbindung zwischen Nebenhaus und dem Nachbarn herstellt.

Aus diesem eingefaßten Zuschauerraum, beschirmt von einem in der Mitte stehenden mächtigen Baum, wird der Blick des Betrachters unweigerlich durch die Lücke zwischen Haupt- und Nebenhaus in den hochliegenden Garten vor dem Haupthaus gelenkt. Nicht weniger als vier Ebenen staffeln sich hintereinander dort hinauf. Theatralisch, fast so wie in einer minimalistischen Wagner-Inszenierung der Nachkriegszeit, führt eine gegenläufige Treppe ohne Geländer über ein vorgelagertes Podest quer zur Blickrichtung aufwärts. Wer dort hinaufgeht, muß viermal seine Richtung ändern, wobei die beim Gang um die Ecken entstehenden unterschiedlichen Perspektiven auf die Baulichkeiten eine abwechslungsreiche »promenade architecturale« bieten.[7] Der Weg setzt sich auf Höhe des ersten Stockwerks des kleinen Hauses nach hinten in den Garten fort und läuft geradewegs auf einen Terrassenvorsprung zu, der als Sockel für eine Plastik gedacht war. Eiermann hätte dort am liebsten eine große Bronze von Henry Moore aufgestellt, den er als Mitglied der Akademie der Künste in Berlin persönlich kennengelernt hatte. Er begnügte sich letztlich mit einem zunächst als Provisorium gedachten riesigen Baumwurzelstrunk, einem skulpturalen Naturgebilde, das, auf den Kopf gestellt, die Assoziation an ein korinthisches Kapitell hervorruft.[8] Den höchsten Punkt dieser architektonisch durchgestalteten Landschaft bildet die oberste Terrasse mit ihrem hervortretenden Podest vor der Längsfront, weit im Hintergrund, aber mit einigem Abstand von der Straße aus immer noch sichtbar. Im Sommer war sie von Segeltuchvorhängen an dünnen Gestängen umhegt, die im geschlossenen Zustand ein vom Haus betretbares »Außenzimmer« bildeten, das nicht eingesehen werden konnte. Im

1. Egon Eiermann vor seinem Haus in Baden–Baden, um 1965. (Photo: Fee Schlapper. saai.)
2. Egon Eiermann, Haus Eiermann, Baden-Baden, Blick auf Atelier- und Haupthaus. (Photo: Horstheinz Neuendorff. saai.)

1. Egon Eiermann in front of his own house in Baden-Baden, ca. 1965. (Photo: Fee Schlapper. saai.)
2. Egon Eiermann, Eiermann House, Baden-Baden, view of studio building and main building. (Photo: Horstheinz Neuendorff. saai.)

Gerhard Kabierske

Simple or complex? The Eiermann House in Baden-Baden – a *Gesamtkunstwerk*

He wanted to build a simple house for himself, a building that, additively arranged, would offer each member of his family their own little house. The floor plans were to correspond to the functional processes of daily life, the form was to be stringently developed from the construction and even the smallest detail was to be well thought out and harmoniously integrated into the whole, since »the detail is what is actually noble in architecture«.[1]

The clear guiding principles of the architect Egon Eiermann, which he eloquently and charismatically propagated in his teaching to the students at the Technische Hochschule of Karlsruhe, were also to form the basis for the design of his own home. With the slogan »We are no painters, we are no sculptors, we are architects«, he tried to convey a specific self-consciousness of the rational architect who wisely brings together all concerns in building and who sets himself apart from the subjectivity of the visual artist.[2] But does the Eiermann House in Baden-Baden really explain itself as a particularly demonstrative object of his personal design solely in terms of functionality, rationality, clarity, appropriateness and coherence in every detail, in terms of those concepts with which the architect himself repeatedly sought to explain his buildings as the result of logical architectural thinking? Brigitte Eiermann, the architect's former pupil and wife – herself an architect, co-builder and co-inhabitant – restricts herself to this view of her husband in her description of the recently completed new building. There is talk of the discipline of the floor plans, of their obvious legibility in the exterior views, of the orientation of the buildings according to the points of the compass and of the »simple structure« or simply of the purpose of the balconies in front of the windows for cleaning the large panes of glass.[3] But already in 1963, when the building magazine *Architektur und Wohnform* published the explanatory text, which Brigitte Eiermann also contributed, a different tone resonates: Almost excusing her husband, she states that it was not a »very simple« house after all, because »it happened to the ardent lover of architecture to create a highly differentiated and very precious structure« during the planning phase.[4] She even tries to capture the aura of the building, which is difficult to describe and in a certain way out of time, with Asian wisdom from Lao Tzu: »Heavy and light complete each other, long and short shape each other, high and low reverse each other, before and after follow each other«.[5] Poetically, this is meant to describe in contrasting terminology what cannot be expressed.

In fact, the building does not present itself by no means as »simple« to today's viewer. Even when approaching via the main access of the street »Krippenhof«, the contrast to the neighbouring estate houses and bungalows that were built almost at the same time could not be greater, just as it is to the cold white boxes that have since replaced them and supposedly want to be »Bauhaus style«. Even from a distance in the flight of the road at the end of the cul-de-sac, the eye is caught by an unusual house. Form, materiality and colour do not correspond to the usual. Arriving at the relatively wide forecourt, which also serves as a public turning area for vehicles, a spatially complex scenery unfolds that has stage-setting qualities: a residential building consisting of two separate structures, standing at right angles to each other, closely interlocked with walls and terraces, »house and annex«, as Eiermann and his wife repeatedly referred to it with deliberately sober modesty.[6] On the left, the large main building rises up gable side on to the viewer and recedes far into the depths. Across in front, the smaller building stands in the way like a gatehouse, shielding a stately home from the public. But instead of a courtyard, the large driveway on the ground floor leads into a half-open double garage. Only at second glance do the large differences in terrain become apparent. The terrain rises sharply to the left and to the rear, the natural topography having been completely altered by human hand. Everything here is terraced, which lends monumentality to the buildings grouped into it, consisting of substructures and structures growing out of them. The forecourt is dug down to a flat level, an enormous ivy-covered quarry stone wall of local red sandstone, the only remnant of the old cot courtyard, intercepts the slope. Like a »repoussoir« in old paintings, the wall in the foreground creates spatial depth as a backdrop pushed in from the side. The fact that the large building is aligned in the same direction reinforces the pull into the depth. On the right of the picture, on the valley side, the scene is bordered by a low wall, which, angled in a hook-like manner, creates the connection between the side building and its neighbour.

From this enclosed auditorium, shielded by a mighty tree standing in the middle, the viewer's gaze is inevitably drawn through the gap between the main building and the side building into the elevated garden in front of the main building. No fewer than four levels are staggered up there one after the other. Theatrically, almost like in a minimalist Wagner production of the post-war period, a counter-rotating staircase without railings leads upwards over an exposed platform situated tranverse to the direction of view. Whoever goes up there has to change direction four times, whereby the different perspectives on the buildings that arise when walking around the corners offer a varied »promenade architecturale«.[7] At the level of the first floor of the side building, the path continues backwards into the garden and runs straight towards a terrace projection that was intended as a plinth for a sculpture. Eiermann would have preferred to place there a large bronze by Henry Moore, whom he had met personally as a member of the Academy of Arts in Berlin. In the end, he settled for a huge tree root stump, initially conceived as a provisional solution, a sculptural natural structure that, turned upside down, evokes the association of a Corinthian capital.[8] The highest point of this architecturally designed landscape is the uppermost terrace with its protruding pedestal in front of the longitudinal front, far in the background but still visible from the street at some distance. In summer, it was enclosed by canvas curtains on thin poles which, when closed, formed an »outer room« that could be entered from the building and could not be seen. When viewed from the street, these curtains on the upper platform again evoked reminiscences of stage and theatre, a memory also evoked by the strange »curtain« on the double garage of the building next door: hanging wooden rods, connected to each other by ropes, can be slid open and closed to the sides via a complicated rod construction. The parked cars always remain visible behind the bars, so this garage does not offer the usual protection, neither against outside temperatures nor against the theft of the vehicles. Eiermann has always justified this solution, which in itself is absurd,

Blick von der Straße weckten diese Vorhänge am oberen Podest erneut Reminiszenzen an Bühne und Theater, eine Erinnerung, die auch der seltsame »Vorhang« an der Doppelgarage des Nebenhauses hervorruft: Hängende Holzstäbe, durch Seile miteinander verbunden, lassen sich über eine komplizierte Stangenkonstruktion zu den Seiten auf- und zuschieben. Die abgestellten Autos bleiben hinter den Stäben immer sichtbar, die Garage bietet daher nicht den gewohnten Schutz, weder gegen Außentemperaturen noch gegen Diebstahl der Fahrzeuge. Eiermann hat diese an sich widersinnige Lösung immer funktional begründet: Aufgrund drohender Schwitzwasserbildung an den Fahrzeugen dürfe eine Garage niemals ein geschlossener Innenraum sein, es sei denn, sie wäre beheizt.[9] Letztlich ist der Einfall mit den Stäben aber nichts anderes als eine überaus ästhetisch gelungene Variation des Themas Geschlossenheit und Offenheit, das am Haus durchgespielt wird. Die hermetische Geschlossenheit von Substruktionen, Giebelwänden und Straßenfassaden aus einheitlich gemauerten Backsteinwänden steht im Kontrast zur großen Öffnung der Garage und der raumgroßen Befensterung darüber, vor allem aber zur Auflösung der gesamten Gartenfront des Haupthauses in Fensterelemente mit großen Glasflächen. Kontraste sind es generell, die den Charakter dieser Architektur maßgeblich prägen: Die Massivität der Wände steht gegen die Leichtigkeit des hauchdünn wirkenden, flach geneigten und extrem weit überstehenden Faserzementdachs sowie gegen das für Eiermann charakteristische »spirrige« Metallgestänge des Sonnenschutzes, das vor den Fensterfronten zusammen mit den auskragenden Balkonen und den Sonnensegeln eine zweite filigrane Fassadenschicht bildet. Auch die derbe Rustikalität der ruinös belassenen historischen Bruchsteinwand des Vorgängerbaus steht im Widerspruch zu der sehr präzise ausgeführten Mauerungstechnik der Backsteinwände des Neubaus. Genauso kontrastreich wie außergewöhnlich ist die Farbigkeit der Architektur: Alle Mauern sind, in der Entstehungszeit völlig ungewöhnlich, dunkel gehalten, anthrazit, fast schwarz, die Backsteine mit einer schlämmenden Farbe überstrichen, ein Fond, der das rötliche Kiefernholz der bündig in die Fassaden eingepaßten Fensterelemente und der feingliedrigen Sparren der Dachkonstruktion aus amerikanischer Oregon Pine, einer besonders harzhaltigen Kiefernart, zu außergewöhnlicher Leuchtkraft bringt. Gegen das Anthrazit der Mauerflächen führen die weiß gestrichenen Gestänge, die mit Seilen daran befestigten Sonnensegel aus weißem Leintuch sowie die ebenfalls weiß gestrichenen Untersichten der Dachüberstände ein stark abstechendes graphisches Eigenleben.

Nachts wird die Szenerie dank einer ausgeklügelten Regie vollends zu einer artifiziellen Traumwelt aus Licht und Schatten. Die schwarzen geschlossenen Wände verschwinden in der Dunkelheit der Nacht, während die helle Innenbeleuchtung die Öffnungen scharfkantig in Erscheinung treten läßt. Das von innen nach außen fallende Licht sowie die außen angebrachten spotlightartigen Scheinwerfer lassen das Gestänge, die Dachuntersichten, die Sonnensegel und Vorhänge surreal aus dem Dunkel aufscheinen. Schlaglichtartige Lichtkegel auf der Bruchsteinwand, auf dem Treppenpodest und der Gartenplastik machen die Bühnenästhetik komplett.

Nein, »einfach« ist am Haus Eiermann nichts; es ist im Sinne von Robert Venturi, dem Apologeten der Postmodrne, ein Musterbeispiel für Komplexität und Widerspruch.[10] Dieses Haus ist eine grandiose künstlerische Inszenierung mit geradezu manieristisch überspitzten Einfällen, ein individuelles Gesamtkunstwerk mit vielen Konnotationen. Rein der Funktion gehorcht hier nichts, oder wie wäre es erklärbar, daß der mit viel gestalterischem Aufwand geradezu pathetisch arrangierte Treppenaufgang keineswegs den Hauptzugang zum Haus bildet? Der zieht an anderer Stelle nochmals ganz andere ästhetische Register.

Eiermann baut Wohnhäuser

An den Bau eines eigenen Hauses mit demonstrativem Anspruch, wie es seit der Renaissance zum Selbstverständnis eines sich profilieren wollenden Architekten gehörte und wie es auch manche seiner Vorgänger auf Lehrstühlen an der Karlsruher Bauschule angestrebt hatten, konnte Egon Eiermann nicht denken, als er 1947 dank der Initiative von Otto Ernst Schweizer zum Architekturprofessor an die Technische Hochschule Karlsruhe berufen wurde. Zu schlecht waren die Bedingungen der ersten Nachkriegsjahre, Stadt und Hochschule waren zerstört, die Reparatur des Allernötigsten stand im Vordergrund. Für ihn, der 1945 in Berlin vor den Trümmern seiner bisherigen beruflichen Existenz gestanden und zunächst in Buchen im Odenwald, der Heimat seines Vaters, untergekommen war, war es schwierig genug, beim Umzug nach Karlsruhe zwei Jahre später überhaupt eine bescheidene erste Unterkunft zu finden. Als Büro mußte zunächst ein Raum im teilzerstörten Architekturgebäude der Hochschule genügen, in dem bei Regen das Wasser von den Decken tropfte. Auch seine Familiensituation war weiterhin von Kriegsumständen geprägt. Seit 1940 mit seiner ersten Frau Charlotte verheiratet und 1942 Vater des Sohnes Andreas geworden, hatte er nach den ersten schweren Bombenangriffen auf Berlin in weiser Voraussicht Frau und Sohn weit entfernt von der Hauptstadt in Volkertshausen untergebracht, einem Dorf im südbadischen Hegau in der Nähe zur Schweizer Grenze. Die Trennung sollte sich bis Ende der 1940er Jahre hinziehen, da Eiermann dort für Frau und Kind die Wohnsituation und die Versorgungslage als gesicherter erachtete. Ein eigenes Haus für die Familie schien unerreichbar, auch wenn Eiermann 1946 seiner Frau, die auf eine baldige Familienzusammenführung drängte, zum Trost eine Grundrißskizze geschickt hatte, um ihr zu zeigen, wie er sich ein gemeinsames Zuhause in einer besseren Zukunft in Buchen vorstellte.[11]

Das damals aktuelle Problem, eine Wohnung im Winter warm zu bekommen, läßt sich selbst an dieser Skizze ablesen: Die Raumdisposition im Wohnraum ist auf einen großen offenen Kamin ausgerichtet und im Schlafbereich, in dem die Einzelbetten der Eltern und des Sohnes nur kojenartig voneinander getrennt sind, auf eine Mauernische mit einem großen Ofen. Im kleinen Bad hätte es nur eine Dusche gegeben. Ansonsten wäre der Bau allerdings recht repräsentativ ausgefallen, bungalowartig und lang gestreckt, mit Bruchsteinwänden aus dem lokalen roten Sandstein nach Norden zu geschlossen, nur an wenigen Stellen von schießschartenähnlichen Öffnungen unterbrochen, während sich nach Süden die Räume mit einer weitgehenden Verglasung zum Garten beziehungsweise zu einem Gartenhof mit Teich hin öffnen sollten. Selbst für die große Küche war ein Fenster von Wand zu Wand vorgesehen – 1946 in heizungstechnischer Hinsicht ein Unding. Ebenso wäre zu diesem Zeitpunkt die Beschaffung von so viel Glas

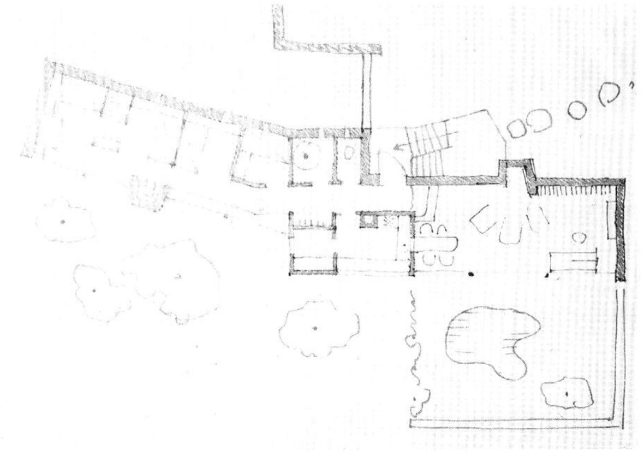

3. Egon Eiermann, Skizze für ein eigenes Wohnhaus in Buchen, 1946. (saai.)
4. Egon Eiermann, Haus Hesse, Berlin-Lankwitz, 1931/1932. (Photo: Arthur Köster. Annemarie Jaeggi (Hg.), *Egon Eiermann (1904 bis 1970). Die Kontinuität der Moderne*, Ausstellungskatalog, Karlsruhe/Berlin 2004, S. 118.)
5. Egon Eiermann, Haus Steingroever, Berlin-Charlottenburg, 1936/37. (Photo: Eberhard Troeger. saai.)

3. Egon Eiermann, sketch for a house of his own in Buchen, 1946. (saai.)
4. Egon Eiermann, Hesse House, Berlin-Lankwitz, 1931/1932. (Photo: Arthur Köster. Annemarie Jaeggi (ed.), *Egon Eiermann (1904 bis 1970). Die Kontinuität der Moderne*, Exhibition catalogue, Karlsruhe/Berlin 2004, p.118.)
5. Egon Eiermann, Steingroever House, Berlin-Charlottenburg, 1936/37. (Photo: Eberhard Troeger. saai.)

in functional terms: Due to the threat of condensation on the vehicles, a garage should never be a closed interior, unless it was heated.[9] Ultimately, however, the idea with the bars is nothing more than an extremely aesthetically successful variation on the theme of enclosure and openness that is played out on the building. The hermetic enclosure of substructures, gable walls and street façades made of uniform brick walls contrasts with the large opening of the garage and the room-sized windows above it, but above all with the dissolution of the entire garden front of the main building into window elements with large glass surfaces. It is contrasts in general that decisively shape the character of this architecture: The solidity of the walls contrasts with the lightness of the seemingly wafer-thin, flatly pitched and extremely overhanging fibre cement roof, as well as with Eiermann's characteristic »spiralling« metal sunshade rods, which, together with the cantilevered balconies and the awnings, form a second filigree layer of façade in front of the window fronts. The rough rusticity of the ruinously left historical quarry stone wall of the previous building also contrasts with the very precisely executed masonry technique of the brick walls of the new building. The colour scheme of the architecture is just as contrasting as it is extraordinary: all the walls are kept dark, anthracite, almost black, completely unusual in the time of their construction, the bricks painted over with a muddy colour, a background that brings the reddish pine of the window elements fitted flush into the façades and the delicate rafters of the roof construction made of American Oregon pine, a particularly resinous type of pine, to extraordinary luminosity. Against the anthracite of the wall surfaces, the white-painted poles, the awnings made of white sheeting attached to them with ropes and the white-painted soffits of the roof overhangs take on a striking graphic life of their own.

At night, the scenery becomes an artificial dream world of light and shadow thanks to a cleverly devised direction. The black closed walls disappear in the darkness of the night, while the bright interior lighting makes the openings appear sharp-edged. The light falling from the inside to the outside as well as the spotlight-like floodlights mounted on the outside make the frame, the soffits, the awnings and curtains appear surreal out of the darkness. Spotlight-like cones of light on the quarry stone wall, on the stair landing and on the garden sculpture complete the stage aesthetic.

No, there is nothing »simple« about the Eiermann House; in the spirit of Robert Venturi, the apologist of post-modernism, it is a prime example of complexity and contradiction.[10] This house is a grandiose artistic production featuring almost manneristically exaggerated ideas, an individual *Gesamtkunstwerk* with many connotations. Nothing here obeys pure function, or how could it be explained that the staircase, arranged almost pathetically with a great deal of creative effort, is by no means the main access to the house? A very different aesthetic tone is struck elsewhere.

Eiermann builds houses

When Egon Eiermann was appointed professor of architecture at the Technische Hochschule of Karlsruhe in 1947, thanks to the initiative of Otto Ernst Schweizer, he could not even think of building his own house with a demonstrative claim, as had been part of the self-image of an architect who wanted to make a name for himself since the Renaissance and as some of his predecessors in the chair of architecture at the Karlsruhe building school had aspired to. The conditions of the first post-war years were too bad; the city and the Hochschule had been destroyed, and the focus was on repairing the bare necessities. For him, who had been faced with the ruins of his previous professional existence in Berlin in 1945 and had initially found accommodation in Buchen in the Odenwald, his father's home, it was difficult enough to find even modest initial accommodation when he moved to Karlsruhe two years later. For the time being, a room in the partially destroyed architecture building of the university, where water dripped from the ceilings when it rained, had to suffice as an office. His family situation also continued to be shaped by wartime circumstances. Married to his first wife Charlotte since 1940 and father of their son Andreas in 1942, he had wisely placed his wife and son far away from the capital in Volkertshausen, a village in the Hegau region of southern Baden near the Swiss border, after the first heavy bombing raids on Berlin. The separation was to last until the end of the 1940s, as Eiermann considered the housing situation and the supply situation for his wife and child to be more secure here. A house of their own for the family seemed unattainable, even though in 1946 Eiermann had sent his wife, who was pressing for an early family reunion, a ground plan sketch as a consolation to show her how he imagined a home together in a better future in Buchen.[11]

The then current problem of getting a flat warm in winter can be seen even in this sketch: The spatial disposition in the living room is oriented towards a large open fireplace and in the sleeping area, where the single beds of the parents and the son are only separated from each other like bunks, towards a wall niche with a large stove. In the small bathroom there would only have been a shower. Otherwise, however, the building would have been quite representative, bungalow-like and elongated, with quarry stone walls made of the local red sandstone, closed to the north, interrupted only in a few places by openings similar to embrasures, while to the south the rooms were to open up with extensive glazing to the garden or to a garden courtyard with a pond. Even the large kitchen was to have a window from wall to wall – an unthinkable idea in 1946 from the point of view of heating technology. Likewise, the procurement of so much glass would simply have been impossible at that time. It was and remained a »dream house«.

With this design sketch, Eiermann was obviously taking up the planning and construction of single-family houses, which had become his trademark in his Berlin work of the 1930s.[12] Commissions for industrial plants such as the Auer-Gesellschaft in Berlin, the Total-Werke in Apolda or the Märkische Metallbau in Oranienburg did not begin until 1938, when the war economy was accelerating. After completing his studies at the Technische Hochschule in Berlin-Charlottenburg, which was mainly influenced by the teaching personality of Hans Poelzig, and after his experiences as an employed architect at the Karstadt department stores' in Hamburg as well as at the Berlin BEWAG, his first residential building, Hesse in Berlin-Lankwitz, built together with his office partner Fritz Jaenecke in 1931/32, already attracted attention. The one-storey building with a flat roof, an outer skin of bricks in the Prüss bond and a »flowing« opening of the living space to the terrace was influenced by Mies

schlichtweg unmöglich gewesen. Es war und blieb ein »Traumhaus«.

Ganz offensichtlich knüpfte Eiermann mit dieser Entwurfsskizze an die Planung und den Bau von Einfamilienhäusern an, die im Berliner Schaffen der 1930er Jahre zu seinem Markenzeichen geworden waren.[12] Aufträge für Industrieanlagen wie die Auer-Gesellschaft in Berlin, die Total-Werke in Apolda oder den Märkischen Metallbau in Oranienburg setzten erst 1938 mit der Forcierung der Kriegswirtschaft ein. Nach Abschluß seines Studiums an der Technischen Hochschule Berlin-Charlottenburg, das vor allem durch die Lehrerpersönlichkeit von Hans Poelzig geprägt war, und nach den Erfahrungen als angestellter Architekt beim Warenhaus Karstadt in Hamburg sowie an der Berliner BEWAG sorgte bereits sein erstes zusammen mit seinem Büropartner Fritz Jaenecke 1931/32 errichtetes Wohnhaus Hesse in Berlin-Lankwitz für Aufmerksamkeit. Der einstöckige Bau mit flachem Dach, einer Außenhaut aus Backsteinen im Prüss-Verband sowie einer »fließenden« Öffnung des Wohnraums zur Terrasse hin ist von Mies van der Rohe beeinflußt.[13] Und umgekehrt war es Mies, der seine Schüler als Leiter des Berliner Bauhauses kurz vor dessen erzwungener Schließung darauf hinwies, sich diesen interessanten Neubau in der Nachbarschaft genauer anzuschauen. Knapp zwanzig weitere Einfamilienhäuser oder Planungen dafür sollten bis 1942 folgen. Sie sind alle in den westlichen Villenvororten von Berlin und im angrenzenden Babelsberg gelegen, wo Eiermann selbst aufgewachsen war, in Kindheit und Jugend wichtige Prägungen empfangen hatte und wo sich später Beziehungen zu potenziellen Bauherren entwickelten. Der 1904 Geborene hatte in der Nähe zur elterlichen Wohnung nicht nur das Entstehen und Wachsen des UFA-Filmgeländes erlebt, sondern auch die rasante Entwicklung der Villenkolonie Neu-Babelsberg, wo sich eine vermögende Berliner Gesellschaft vor und nach dem Ersten Weltkrieg repräsentative Landhäuser errichten ließ. Hier konnte Eiermann den Bau der Erstlingswerke von Mies van der Rohe im Stil der Zeit »um 1800« miterleben. Darüber hinaus hatte er durch die Schulbekanntschaft mit der Tochter von Peter Behrens Zugang zum Haus und Architekturatelier des damaligen Stararchitekten, bei dem die kommenden Größen der modernen Architektur vor dem Ersten Weltkrieg ein und aus gingen.[14] Gerne erzählte Eiermann die Anekdote, er habe als frecher Knabe von einem Kirschbaum aus Kerne auf Gropius, Mies und den späteren Le Corbusier gespuckt, als diese im Behrensschen Garten miteinander diskutiert hätten. Doch diese Schilderung ist eine Legende, da die drei Avantgardisten nie gemeinsam bei Behrens gearbeitet hatten. Sie beleuchtet aber durchaus, in welchem baukünstlerisch inspirierenden Umfeld der junge Eiermann aufwuchs und moderne Wohnkultur erlebte.[15]

Die Baupolitik der Nationalsozialisten, mit denen der 30jährige Berufsanfänger ab 1933 konfrontiert war, kollidierte mit seinen Vorstellungen einer auf Baukultur zielenden Moderne im Sinne seines Lehrers Poelzig, auch wenn der junge Architekt Distanz zum »weißen« Funktionalismus der späten 1920er Jahre hielt und mit dem Bauhaus lebenslang nichts zu tun haben wollte. Eiermann war jedoch nicht bereit, sich von seinen Überzeugungen zu distanzieren. Er weigerte sich, Parteimitglied zu werden, emigrierte aber auch nicht wie sein Studienkollege und zeitweiliger Büropartner Jaenecke. Zu fest war die Verwurzelung in seinem Berliner Milieu. Das zwang ihn bis 1945 zu einer Gratwanderung zwischen Distanzierung und Anpassung.[16] Öffentliche Großaufträge, wie sie sein im NS-Staat mächtig gewordener Studienkollege Albert Speer als Generalbauinspekteur zu vergeben hatte, blieben ihm verwehrt, mit Ausnahme der temporären Inszenierung der Maschinenhalle und des Kinoraums auf der NS-Propagandaausstellung »Gebt mir vier Jahre Zeit« von 1937.[17] Bei der Halle konnte er sich, ohne auf Kritik zu stoßen, einer geradezu konstruktivistischen Ästhetik der 1920er Jahre bedienen, während der luzide und leichte Kinosaal mit seinem dünnen Stützenwald offensichtlich von Heinrich Tessenow beeinflußt war, einem seiner Lehrer an der Berliner Technischen Hochschule. Allein bei einem Auftrag für einen Kasernenbau in Rathenow, den er später wohlweislich verschwieg, verleugnete er zur Sicherung der Weiterbeschäftigung von Mitarbeitern seine eigentliche Handschrift zugunsten eines regionalistisch-traditionellen Stils.[18] Eine Nische für ein Entwerfen nach seinem Gusto bot ihm neben dem Industriebau vor allem die Spezialisierung auf Einfamilienhäuser. Bauherren, die ein Haus abseits des offiziellen Geschmacks zwischen monumentalem Neoklassizismus und Heimatschutz bevorzugten, fanden sich in den Villengebieten des Berliner Westens auch im »Dritten Reich«. Sie schätzten offenbar Eiermanns Bereitschaft und Fähigkeit, ihre persönlichen Wünsche mit seinen formalen Vorstellungen in Einklang zu bringen.[19] Die Palette der individuellen Lösungen ist deshalb von Haus zu Haus breit, sei es in Dimensionen und Proportionen, in ungewöhnlichen Grundrißdispositionen oder Raum- und Materialwirkungen. Nichts ist Routine, die Häuser sind bis ins Detail hinein durchdacht und überzeugen bei aller Einfachheit der Mittel. Da Eiermann im Hinblick auf Dachformen nie doktrinär die Flachdachideologie der 1920er Jahre vertrat und auch bei Fassadenmaterialien mit der bevorzugten Verwendung von Backstein nicht aneckte, konnte er eine ganze Reihe von Einfamilienhäusern realisieren. Fehlender Dachüberstand, große Fensterformate oder zu flache Dachneigungen riefen jedoch immer wieder Widerspruch bei den Baugenehmigungsbehörden hervor, den Eiermann geschickt konterte, ohne sich zu verbiegen. Sein Meisterwerk der Zeit, das 1939–43 errichtete Haus Vollberg, wurde nur genehmigt, weil das avantgardistisch gruppierte, flach ausgestreckte Gebäude mit weit überstehendem Faserzementdach von der Straße her nicht einsehbar war.[20] Ein Vorentwurf für ein Grundstück direkt an einer Straße war wegen seines Aussehens noch kategorisch abgelehnt worden.

Wenn der Architekt auch keine Chance hatte, daß seine Bauten in den zahlreichen offiziellen Veröffentlichungen für das »Bauen im Neuen Reich« aufgenommen wurden, so wagten doch Fachzeitschriften wie die *Bauwelt*, *Westermanns Monatshefte für Baukunst* oder *Moderne Bauformen* ihre Publikation. Für Eiermann sollten diese klandestin verbreiteten Leistungen nach 1945 im Hinblick auf seine Karriere sehr dienlich werden. Daß sich 1946/47 gleich vier Hochschulen darum bemühten, den Architekten dieser Bauten als Lehrer zu gewinnen, war diesen Artikeln geschuldet.

Ausgerechnet der Weltkrieg und seine Folgen hatten Eiermann aber auch Möglichkeiten eröffnet, für Wohnnutzungen zu planen. 1942, die alliierten Luftangriffe auf Berlin häuften sich, erhielt er den Auftrag zum Bau der Krankenhaus-Sonderanlage im märkischen Kiefernwald von Beelitz-Heilstätten unweit von Potsdam, das zunächst Platz für die Auslagerung zerstörter Kliniken, ab Ende 1943 aber auch Unterkunft für ausgebombte Ber-

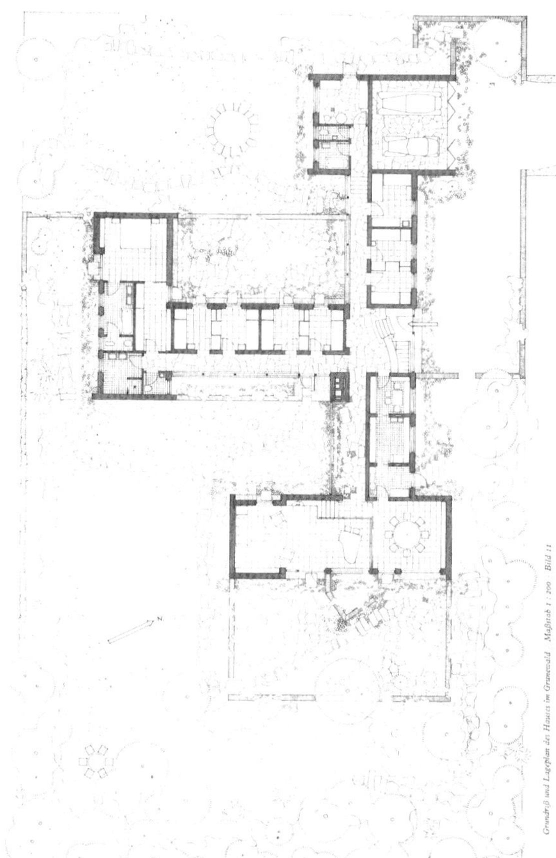

6. Egon Eiermann, Haus Vollberg, Berlin-Grunewald, 1939–43. (Photo: Eberhard Troeger. saai.)
7. Egon Eiermann, Haus Vollberg, Berlin-Grunewald, Grundriß. (*Bauwelt*, 1942, H. 39/40, S. 5. saai.)
8. Ausweichbüro von Egon Eiermann in Beelitz-Heilstätten, 1943/44, Gemeinschaftsraum. (Photo: Eberhard Troeger. saai.)
9. Egon Eiermann, Häuser der Siedlernotgemeinschaft in Hettingen / Odenwald, 1946.

6. Egon Eiermann, Vollberg House, Berlin-Grunewald, 1939–43. (Photo: Eberhard Troeger. saai.)
7. Egon Eiermann, Vollberg House, Berlin-Grunewald, floor plan. (*Bauwelt*, 1942, no. 39/40, p. 5. saai.)
8. Alternate office of Egon Eiermann in Beelitz-Heilstätten, 1943/44, community room. (Photo: Eberhard Troeger. saai.)
9. Egon Eiermann, houses of a settlers' emergency community in Hettingen / Odenwald, 1946.

van der Rohe.[13] And conversely, it was Mies who, as director of the Berlin Bauhaus shortly before its forced closure, advised his students to take a closer look at this interesting new building in the neighbourhood. Almost twenty more single-family houses or plans for them were to follow until 1942. They were all located in the western villa suburbs of Berlin and in neighbouring Babelsberg, where Eiermann himself had grown up, had received important impressions in childhood and youth, and where relationships with potential builders later developed. Born in 1904, Eiermann had not only witnessed the emergence and growth of the UFA film complex in the vicinity of his parents' home, but also the rapid development of the Neu-Babelsberg villa colony, where wealthy Berlin society had prestigious country houses built before and after the First World War. Here Eiermann was able to witness the construction of Mies van der Rohe's first works in the style of the period »around 1800«. In addition, through his school acquaintance with the daughter of Peter Behrens, he had access to the house and architectural studio of the star architect of the time, where the future greats of modern architecture came and went before the First World War.[14] Eiermann liked to tell the anecdote that as a cheeky boy he spat seeds from a cherry tree at Gropius, Mies and the later Le Corbusier when they were discussing with each other in Behrens' garden. But this account is a legend, since the three avant-garde artists never worked together at Behrens'. It does, however, shed light on the inspiring architectural environment in which the young Eiermann grew up and experienced modern residential culture.[15]

The building policies of the National Socialists, with which the 30-year-old professional was confronted from 1933 onwards, collided with his ideas of a modernism aimed at building culture in the spirit of his teacher Poelzig, even though the young architect kept his distance from the »white« functionalism of the late 1920s and wanted nothing to do with the Bauhaus for the rest of his life. Eiermann, however, was not prepared to distance himself from his convictions. He refused to become a party member, but did not emigrate like his fellow student and temporary office partner Jaenecke. He was too firmly rooted in his Berlin milieu. This forced him to walk a tightrope between distancing and adaptation until 1945.[16] He was denied major public contracts, such as those awarded to his fellow student Albert Speer, who had become powerful in the Nazi state, as general building inspector, with the exception of the temporary staging of the machine hall and the cinema room at the Nazi propaganda exhibition »Give me four years' time« in 1937.[17] In the case of the hall, Eiermann was able to make use of an almost constructivist aesthetic of the 1920s without encountering criticism, while the lucid and light cinema hall with its thin forest of columns was obviously influenced by Heinrich Tessenow, one of his teachers at the Berlin Technische Hochschule. Only in the case of a commission for a barracks in Rathenow, which he later wisely concealed, did he disavow his actual signature in favour of a regionalist-traditional style in order to secure the continued employment of staff.[18] In addition to industrial construction, specialising in single-family houses offered him a niche for designing to his liking. Builders who preferred a house outside the official taste between monumental neoclassicism and *Heimatschutz* could be found in the villa areas of Berlin's West, even in the »Third Reich«. They obviously appreciated Eiermann's willingness and ability to harmonise their personal wishes with his formal ideas.[19] The range of individual solutions is therefore broad from house to house, be it in dimensions and proportions, in unusual ground plan dispositions or spatial and material effects. Nothing is routine; the houses are thought out down to the last detail and are convincing for all their simplicity of means. Since Eiermann never doctrinally advocated the flat-roof ideology of the 1920s with regard to roof forms and also did not take offence at façade materials with his preferred use of brick, he was able to realise a whole series of single-family houses. However, a lack of roof overhang, large window formats or roof pitches that were too flat repeatedly provoked objections from the building permit authorities, which Eiermann cleverly countered without bending. His masterpiece of the time, Haus Vollberg, built in 1939–43, was only approved because the avant-garde structured, flatly stretched out building with a far overhanging fibre-cement roof could not be seen from the street.[20] A preliminary design for a property directly on a street had still been categorically rejected because of its appearance.

Even if the architect had no chance of his buildings being included in the numerous official publications for »Building in the New Reich«, trade journals such as *Bauwelt*, *Westermanns Monatshefte für Baukunst* or *Moderne Bauformen* dared to publish them. For Eiermann, these clandestinely disseminated achievements were to become very useful for his career after 1945. The fact that in 1946/47 four universities tried to recruit the architect of these buildings as a teacher was due to these articles.

Of all things, however, the world war and its aftermath had also opened up opportunities for Eiermann to plan for residential use. In 1942, as the Allied air raids on Berlin increased, he was commissioned to build the special hospital complex in the pine forest of Beelitz-Heilstätten not far from Potsdam, which was initially to provide space for the removal of destroyed clinics, but from the end of 1943 was also to provide accommodation for bombed-out Berlin Reich authorities.[21] Not only did Eiermann secure exemption from military service for himself and his staff with this major project in the midst of the »total war«, it was also connected with the possibility of creating a temporary building for his local office in Beelitz.[22] Eiermann was not satisfied with one of the usual standard barracks. Even under the most adverse conditions of material procurement, he succeeded in realising an individually planned wooden house of high aesthetic standards, for which the furniture was even specially made. It housed not only an open-plan room with drawing tables and a separate executive bedroom, but also overnight accommodation. Small sleeping cells for five people were lined up along a corridor that offered space for personal clothing and utensils behind curtains. This was followed by sanitary rooms and a kitchen, as well as a communal area where people could live and eat together around the centre of an open fireplace surrounded by armchairs. If you like, it was the first dwelling of his own that he could build alone according to his personal ideas, since Eiermann's flats in Berlin had always been in old buildings up to that point. This island in the midst of an increasingly threatening outside world existed for only a few months, only to go up in flames when the Russian troops advanced on Berlin.

As hopeless as the situation seemed at first after the adventurous flight to the Odenwald, Eiermann soon managed to create a building and living culture there as

liner Reichsbehörden bieten sollte.[21] Nicht nur, daß Eiermann mit diesem Großprojekt inmitten des »totalen Krieges« für sich und seine Mitarbeiter die Freistellung vom Kriegsdienst sicherte, verbunden war damit auch die Möglichkeit, in Beelitz ein provisorisches Gebäude für sein örtliches Büro zu erstellen.[22] Eiermann gab sich nicht mit einer der üblichen Normbaracken zufrieden. Selbst unter widrigsten Bedingungen der Materialbeschaffung gelang es ihm, ein individuell geplantes Holzhaus von hohem ästhetischem Anspruch zu realisieren, für das sogar eigens das Mobiliar angefertigt wurde. Es beherbergte nicht nur einen Großraum mit Zeichentischen und ein separates Chefzimmer, sondern auch Übernachtungsmöglichkeiten. An einem Flur, der hinter Vorhängen Raum für persönliche Kleidung und Utensilien bot, reihten sich kleine Schlafzellen für fünf Personen. Es schlossen sich Sanitärräume und eine Küche an sowie ein Gemeinschaftsbereich, in dem man um den Mittelpunkt eines von Sesseln umstandenen offenen Kamins gemeinsam wohnen und essen konnte. Wenn man so will, war es eine erste eigene Behausung, die er allein nach seinen persönlichen Vorstellungen errichten konnte, da Eiermanns Wohnungen in Berlin sich bislang immer in Altbauten befanden. Diese Insel inmitten einer immer bedrohlicher werdenden Außenwelt existierte freilich nur wenige Monate, um beim Vormarsch der russischen Truppen auf Berlin in Flammen aufzugehen.

So aussichtslos die Situation nach der abenteuerlichen Flucht in den Odenwald zunächst schien, auch dort verstand es Eiermann, trotz größter Einschränkungen durch die Versorgungslage bald wieder eine Bau- und Wohnkultur zu schaffen. Zusammen mit Heinrich Magnagni, dem ungemein engagierten und charismatischen Ortspriester, sowie seinem Berliner Büromitarbeiter Robert Hilgers, der ihm in den Odenwald gefolgt war und zum langjährigen Büropartner avancierte, schuf er dort mit den Häusern der Siedlernotgemeinschaften in Buchen und Hettingen Musterbeispiele einfachen Bauens für Flüchtlinge. In Buchen konnte Eiermann 1946 bis 1948 fünf Einzelhäuser, im benachbarten Hettingen elf Doppelhäuser realisieren, die trotz größter Probleme bei Finanzierung und Materialbeschaffung alles andere als nur ein Notbehelf waren.[23] Da wurde mit Lehmbauweise experimentiert, die in Berlin erfundene und in den 1920er Jahren von Poelzig und seiner Schule gerne verwendete Prüss-Technik der Fassadenverkleidung in Backstein eingeführt, Dachstühle mit Brettersparren konstruiert, aber auch ungewöhnliche Grundrisse mit zum Wohnraum hin offenen Küchen oder separaten Schrankräumen zwischen den Schlafzimmern realisiert. Und bei aller Notwendigkeit des Sparens standen für Eiermann nicht nur funktionale Kriterien im Fokus, sondern auch ästhetische. Proportionen, Materialwirkungen, Farben, die Gestaltung von Fenstern und Türen und Details wie die Treppengeländer im Inneren erfreuen bis heute, leider nur noch an einem weitgehend erhaltenen, vorbildlich sanierten und inzwischen museal genutzten Haus in Hettingen, während alle anderen Häuser bis zur Unkenntlichkeit verstümmelt wurden.

Einfamilienhäuser spielten im Frühwerk Eiermanns eine zentrale Rolle. Umso überraschender ist es, daß sie sich im weiteren Œuvre rar machten. Mit dem Erfolg, der sich mit der Konsolidierung der wirtschaftlichen Verhältnisse nach 1949 einstellte und Eiermann zu einem der bekanntesten Vertreter der modernen Architekturszene in der jungen Bundesrepublik machte, kamen zunehmend bedeutende Aufträge für Großbauten aus der Wirtschaft, die Eiermann neben seiner Lehre vollstes Engagement abverlangten. Ohne vorherige Wettbewerbe wurden ihm die Verwaltungs- und Produktionsbauten der Ciba in Wehr, die Taschentuchweberei in Blumberg, das Verwaltungsgebäude der Vereinigten Seidenwebereien in Krefeld, die Kaufhäuser Merkur in Heilbronn, Reutlingen und Stuttgart, das Verlagsgebäude von Burda-Moden in Offenburg sowie das Verwaltungsgebäude der Essener Steinkohlebergwerke übertragen, um nur die wichtigsten Beispiele der 1950er Jahre zu nennen. Doch nicht nur als Architekt des Wirtschaftswunders machte Eiermann Furore. Seit seiner Gestaltung der Deutschen Abteilung auf der Triennale in Mailand 1954 stieg er zu einem Architekten auf, der mit staatlichen Bauaufgaben die Bundesrepublik nach dem Nationalsozialismus wieder international als Kulturnation präsentieren sollte. Der besonders vom Ausland gefeierte Deutsche Pavillon auf der Weltausstellung in Brüssel 1958, die Deutsche Botschaft in Washington sowie der ebenfalls eminent politisch aufgeladene Wiederaufbau der Kaiser-Wilhelm-Gedächtniskirche im geteilten Berlin ließen ihn zu einer öffentlichen Person von weitreichender Bekanntheit werden.[24]

Da er trotz eines mehrfach erweiterten Büros mit zahlreichen Mitarbeitern bei allen Aufträgen die Fäden selbst in den Händen halten und sich um jedes kleinste Detail kümmern wollte, war die Arbeitsbelastung immens. Bauherren, die sich von ihm ein Wohnhaus wünschten, gab es viele, vor allem aus Professorenkreisen der Technischen Hochschule Karlsruhe und Wissenschaftler des neu gegründeten Karlsruher Kernforschungszentrums. Sie wurden alle abschlägig beschieden. Spielten wirtschaftliche Überlegungen gegenüber kleineren Bauaufgaben dabei sicherlich eine Rolle, so stilisierte Eiermann seine Zurückhaltung gerne mit der besonderen Bürde beim Wohnhausbau: »Mein letztes Wohnhaus entstand 1938. Ich konnte und wollte auch keines mehr bauen. Die Unbekümmertheit der Jugend setzt sich nach meiner Erinnerung leichter hinweg über die Schwierigkeiten einer solchen Aufgabe. Lautet sie doch: Menschen zu verbinden, ihr Leben wertvoll zu machen, Lebensraum zu schenken, Glück zu formen, jetzt älter oder gar alt geworden, weiß man, daß eine Wohnstatt zu bauen das größte Problem ist, weil es das menschlichste ist.« Die Chance, ein Haus von Eiermann zu bekommen, hatte nur, wer in einer besonderen Beziehung zu ihm stand. So entwarf er 1954/55 für den Verleger Woldemar Klein, der gleich nach 1945 als Herausgeber der Avantgardezeitschrift *Das Kunstwerk* bekannt geworden war, einen Anbau an dessen Baden-Badener Haus, ein Werk, das Eiermann jedoch nie zur Publikation freigab. Für Eiermann völlig enttäuschend endete sein Engagement für das Haus des Frankfurter Bankiers Feith.[25] Dessen Frau war eine gute Bekannte aus Berliner Zeiten. Auf einem Grundstück im Villengebiet am Frankfurter Lerchesberg sollte 1958/59 ein typologisch interessantes Haus entstehen, das den besonderen Sicherheitsbedürfnissen des Bauherrn Rechnung trug und sich mit einem Hausmeistertrakt gegen die Straße abschottete. Obwohl die Planung durch das Büro Eiermann bis hin zu den Werkzeichnungen gediehen war, erfolgte die Ausführung durch einen örtlichen Architekten, der derart entscheidende Änderungen vornahm, daß Eiermann fortan jegliche Urheberschaft an diesem Haus bestritt.

Mehr Glück war der Villa Hardenberg in Baden-Baden beschieden, das zu einem Meisterwerk der Baukunst der späten 1950er Jahre werden sollte.[26] Der er-

10. Egon und Brigitte Eiermann in ihrer Wohnung in Karlsruhe-Neureut, 1957. (*Bunte Illustrierte*, Heft 35, 1957, S. 39, Photo: Hans Schlitz. saai.)

10. Egon and Brigitte Eiermann in their apartment in Karlsruhe-Neureut, 1957. (*Bunte Illustrierte*, no. 35, 1957, p. 39, Photo: Hans Schlitz. saai.)

well, despite the greatest restrictions due to the supply situation. Together with Heinrich Magnagni, the immensely committed and charismatic local priest, and his Berlin office assistant Robert Hilgers, who had followed him to the Odenwald and advanced to become his long-time office partner, he created there, with the houses of the settlers' emergency communities in Buchen and Hettingen, prime examples of simple building for refugees. Between 1946 and 1948 Eiermann was able to build five single houses in Buchen, and eleven semi-detached houses in neighbouring Hettingen, which were anything but makeshift despite the greatest problems with financing and material procurement.[23] He experimented with earthen construction, introduced the Prüss technique of façade cladding in brick, invented in Berlin and popularly used by Poelzig and his school in the 1920s, constructed roof trusses with board rafters, and also realised unusual floor plans with kitchens open to the living space or separate closet rooms between the bedrooms. And for all the need to economise, Eiermann focused not only on functional criteria but also on aesthetic ones. Proportions, material effects, colours, the design of windows and doors and details such as the interior stair railings are still pleasing today, unfortunately only in one largely preserved, exemplary renovated house in Hettingen, which is now used as a museum, while all the other houses have been mutilated beyond recognition.

Single-family houses played a central role in Eiermann's early work. It is all the more surprising that they were rare in the rest of his oeuvre. With the success that came with the consolidation of economic conditions after 1949 and made Eiermann one of the best-known representatives of the modern architectural scene in the young Federal Republic, increasingly important commissions for large buildings came from industry, which demanded Eiermann's fullest commitment in addition to his teaching. Without prior competitions, he was commissioned to design the administrative and production buildings of Ciba in Wehr, the handkerchief weaving mill in Blumberg, the administrative building of Vereinigte Seidenwebereien in Krefeld, the Merkur department stores in Heilbronn, Reutlingen and Stuttgart, the publishing building of Burda-Moden in Offenburg and the administrative building of the Essen coal mines, to name only the most important examples of the 1950s. But Eiermann did not only cause a sensation as an architect of the economic miracle. Since his design of the German Department at the Triennale in Milan in 1954, he rose to become an architect who was to use state building commissions to present the Federal Republic of Germany as a cultural nation again internationally after National Socialism. The German Pavilion at the 1958 World's Fair in Brussels, which was particularly celebrated abroad, the German Embassy in Washington and the reconstruction of the Kaiser Wilhelm Memorial Church in divided Berlin, which was also eminently politically charged, made him a public figure of far-reaching renown.[24]

Despite a repeatedly expanded office with numerous employees, he wanted to hold the reins in his own hands and take care of every last detail, so the workload was immense. There were many clients who wanted him to build a house, especially professors from the Technical University of Karlsruhe and scientists from the newly founded Karlsruhe Nuclear Research Centre. They were all turned down. While economic considerations certainly played a role compared to smaller building projects, Eiermann liked to stylise his reticence with the particular burden of building residential buildings: »My last residential building was built in 1938. I could not and did not want to build another one. As I remember it, the carefree attitude of youth is easier to ignore the difficulties of such a task. After all, it is to connect people, to make their lives valuable, to give living space, to shape happiness. Now that you are older or even old, you know that building a home is the greatest problem because it is the most human.« Only those who had a special relationship with Eiermann had a chance of getting one of his houses. In 1954/55, for example, he designed an extension to the Baden-Baden house of the publisher Woldemar Klein, who had become known immediately after 1945 as the editor of the avant-garde magazine *Das Kunstwerk*, a work that Eiermann, however, never released for publication. For Eiermann, his engagement in the house of the Frankfurt banker Feith ended in complete disappointment.[25] Feith's wife was a good acquaintance from his Berlin days. In 1958/59, a typologically interesting house was to be built on a plot of land in the villa area on Frankfurt's Lerchesberg, which took into account the special security needs of the client and sealed itself off from the street with a caretaker's wing. Although the planning by the Eiermann office had progressed to the working drawings, the execution was carried out by a local architect who made such decisive changes that Eiermann henceforth denied any authorship of this house.

The Hardenberg Villa in Baden-Baden, which was to become a masterpiece of late 1950s architecture, was more fortunate.[26] Count von Hardenberg, a successful car dealer from Karlsruhe married to a Princess von Fürstenberg, asked his client Eiermann for advice on his plans to build a new villa on a large plot of land in a prime location in Baden-Baden. He had not been satisfied with the designs of various architects. They got talking and the relationship developed in an almost ideal way, much to Eiermann's delight. The huge house with its T-shaped ground plan, which seems to float flat above the site, was built in close coordination. The hard horizontal dominants of the concrete floor and ceiling slab are relieved of their heaviness and hardness by the recessed, extensive glazing in wooden elements, by the brickwork with red bricks and the white rods of the walkway, which are overgrown with knotweed.

Site search

Egon Eiermann's brilliant rise to the top of the German architectural scene and the financial security that went with it led him in the 1950s to want to finally demonstrate his personal ideas and skills with a house of his own. In addition, family circumstances had changed. After divorcing his first wife Charlotte – the couple, like many in Germany, had not found their way back to each other after the long separation caused by the war and the post-war period – the 50-year-old Eiermann married Brigitte Feyerabendt in 1954, twenty years his junior, a former architecture student who had graduated from Karlsruhe with him four years earlier. In 1956 he became a father a second time with the birth of daughter Anna. A servant's flat in the centre of Karlsruhe, which he moved into after the marriage, soon became too cramped, especially as Eiermann's mother, who was increasingly in need of care, was also to move nearby. In 1956, the family rented a newly built house in Neureut

folgreiche Karlsruher Autohändler Graf von Hardenberg, verheiratet mit einer Prinzessin von Fürstenberg, fragte seinen Kunden Eiermann um Rat wegen seines Neubauvorhabens einer Villa auf einem großen Grundstück in bester Lage in Baden-Baden. Mit den Entwürfen verschiedener Architekten war er nicht zufrieden gewesen. Man kam ins Gespräch, und das Verhältnis entwickelte sich zu Eiermanns Freude in geradezu idealer Weise. In enger Abstimmung entstand das riesige Haus über T-förmigem Grundriß, das flach über dem Areal zu schweben scheint. Den harten horizontalen Dominanten der Fußboden- und Deckenplatte aus Beton wird durch die zurückgesetzte weitgehende Verglasung in Holzelementen, durch die Ausmauerung mit roten Backsteinen und das von Knöterich überwucherte weiße Gestänge des Umgangs die Schwere und Härte genommen.

Grundstückssuche

Der fulminante Aufstieg an die Spitze der bundesdeutschen Architekturszene und damit einhergehend eine gesicherte finanzielle Existenz ließen in Egon Eiermann in den 1950er Jahren die Absicht wachsen, endlich auch mit einem eigenen Wohnhaus seine persönlichen Vorstellungen und sein Können unter Beweis zu stellen. Zudem hatten sich die familiären Verhältnisse geändert. Nach der Scheidung von seiner ersten Frau Charlotte – das Paar hatte wie viele in Deutschland nach der langen Trennung durch Krieg und Nachkriegszeit nicht mehr zueinandergefunden – heiratete der 50jährige Eiermann 1954 die zwanzig Jahre jüngere Brigitte Feyerabendt, eine ehemalige Architekturstudentin, die vier Jahre zuvor in Karlsruhe bei ihm ihr Diplom gemacht hatte. 1956 wurde er mit der Geburt von Tochter Anna ein zweites Mal Vater. Eine nach der Heirat bezogene Dienstwohnung in der Karlsruher Innenstadt wurde bald zu eng, zumal auch die zunehmend pflegebedürftige Mutter von Eiermann in die Nähe ziehen sollte. 1956 mietete die Familie ein neu errichtetes Haus in Neureut bei Karlsruhe, das genug Platz für alle bot. Aufnahmen des Pressephotographen Hans Schlitz, der Eiermann für einen Artikel über den »Stararchitekten« in der *Bunten Illustrierten* 1957 einen Tag lang begleitete, zeigen Einblicke in diese Wohnung, deren Wohnzimmer mit Serienmöbeln ausgestattet war, die Eiermann für die Ausstellung »Wie Wohnen« 1949 entworfen hatte.[27] Der Allerweltsbau, der den Ansprüchen des Architekten nicht genügen konnte, wurde von Anfang an nur als Zwischenlösung betrachtet. In einem Brief beklagte sich Eiermann über das »entsetzliche Milieu« am gesichtslosen Stadtrand, in dem er dort leben müsse, »zwischen amerikanischen Kasernen, Kiesgruben und Niemandsland«.[28] Etwas Eigenes in besserer Umgebung war spätestens mit dem großen Erfolg des Deutschen Pavillons auf der Weltausstellung in Brüssel beschlossene Sache.

Der Blick richtete sich zunächst auf einen Bauplatz in unmittelbarer Nähe zur Technischen Hochschule, wo am Rand des Fasanengartens und neben dem Botanischen Institut ein Areal in Landeseigentum für die Errichtung von Professorenhäusern reserviert war. Rudolf Büchner, ein wichtiger Mitarbeiter Eiermanns aus dessen Berliner Zeit und von ihm 1952 als Lehrer an die Hochschule geholt, hatte dort schon drei Häuser für Lehrstuhlinhaber realisiert.[29] Für ein noch freies Eckgrundstück machte Eiermann 1958 erste Pläne. Er wollte die fast quadratische Parzelle mit einer hohen Mauer umgeben, im Karree sollte das Haus stehen, für das er drei sehr unterschiedliche Ansätze entwickelte. Eine Überlegung sah ein zweigeschossiges Wohnhaus mit Flachdach vor, ein Solitär in der Art der Villa Hardenberg, die andere ein ebenfalls zweigeschossiges, aber gruppiertes Haus mit Satteldach, das ältere Wohnhausentwürfe des Architekten aufgriff. Bei der ungewöhnlichsten Variante sollten sich im Innenbereich zwei parallel gestellte, niedrige eingeschossige Gebäude mit flach geneigten, weit überstehenden und von Pfosten getragenen Dächern ducken, eines zum Wohnen, das andere zum Schlafen – ein fast klösterlicher, gegen die Welt abgeschiedener Bezirk mit einer additiv gefügten, sehr einfachen und leichten Architektur. Das Muster der »Baracke« von Beelitz-Heilstätten war offenbar noch nicht vergessen, und der Einfluß von Mies van der Rohes vitrinenartigem Farnsworth-Haus sowie traditioneller japanischer Häuser unverkennbar. Die strikte Funktionstrennung wäre folgenreich für den Alltag gewesen, hätte man doch immer durchs Freie müssen, um vom einen Haus zum anderen zu gelangen. Weit gedieh das Projekt nicht. Eiermann bekam Bedenken wegen der Nähe zur Hochschule. Eine größere räumliche Distanz zur Architekturfakultät, die er zwar dominierte, die ihm aber auch über Gebühr Kraft kostete, schien ihm geboten. Der Kollege Otto Ernst Schweizer hatte es mit seinem Wohnsitz in Baden-Baden zwanzig Jahre früher schon vorgemacht. Die renommierte Kurstadt, 40 km entfernt, stand 1958 wegen der Villa Hardenberg gerade in seinem Fokus, und so machte sich das Ehepaar dort auf die Suche nach einem geeigneten Bauplatz.

Der Stadtverwaltung unter ihrem Oberbürgermeister Schlapper war daran gelegen, den bekannt gewordenen Architekten an Baden-Baden zu binden und kam ihm entgegen. Aus kommunalem Grundbesitz bot man ihm einen Bauplatz am Krippenhof an, einem bevorzugten Neubauquartier mit nach Südwesten orientierter Hanglage, inklusive Blick ins Oostal, auf den am Hang gegenüberliegenden Kurpark und die von Leo von Klenze erbauten Stourdza-Kapelle. Eine gute Adresse in einer Stadt, die schon seit dem 19. Jahrhundert Kurgäste aus aller Welt anzog. Das historistische Fürstenberg-Denkmal von 1870 und das Sanatorium Dr. Heinsheimer, errichtet 1905 von Hermann Billing und Wilhelm Vittali, hatten in der Nachbarschaft schon bauliche Marksteine gesetzt. Die Domäne Krippenhof war wie das östlich anschließende Herrengut in den 1950er Jahren parzelliert und mit Einfamilienhäusern und kleineren Zweifamilienhäusern bebaut worden, wobei sich die Gebäude allerdings allesamt nicht durch eine besondere architektonische Gestaltung hervortaten – »unteres Mittelmaß«, wie Eiermann in einem Brief an den Oberbürgermeister abschätzig konstatierte.[30]

Das fragliche Grundstück hatte zuvor bislang noch keinen Käufer gefunden, weil es vermutlich als schwierig zu bebauen galt: unregelmäßig geschnitten, nach zwei Seiten hin mit beträchtlichem Gefälle, nach Süden stärker, nach Westen flacher. Der Höhenunterschied zwischen der Nordostecke und der Südwestecke betrug mehr als 7 m, ungünstig für jedes Haus von der Stange. Ungewöhnlich war auch die Erschließung von zwei Seiten, die in der Vorgängerbebauung ihre Ursache hatte. Von Südwesten führt die Straße »Krippenhof« als Sackgasse mit Wendeplatz auf das Areal zu. Davor, weiter südwestlich, zweigt ein Arm der Straße jedoch ab, erklimmt den steilen Hang und führt bergseitig am Grundstück entlang. Die eingangs erwähnte Böschungsmauer

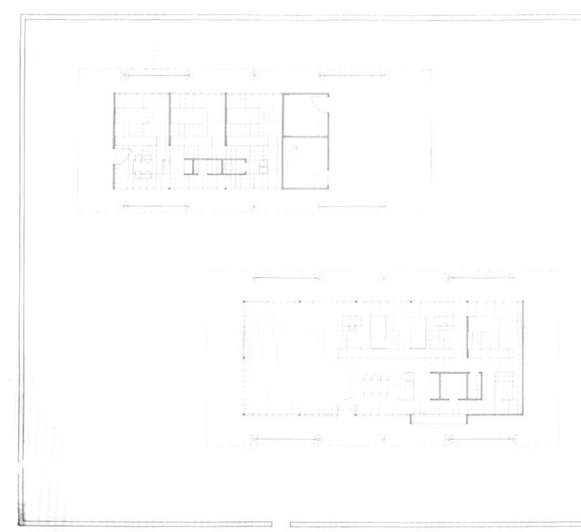

11,12. Egon Eiermann, Entwurfsvarianten für ein eigenes Haus in Karlsruhe, Am Fasanengarten, Ecke Hansjakobstraße, 1958. (saai.)
13. Grundstück Krippenhof 16/18, Baden-Baden vor Beginn der Bauarbeiten mit Resten des alten Krippenhofs, 1958/59. (Photo: Büro Eiermann. saai.)
14. Egon Eiermann, Villa Hardenberg, Baden-Baden, 1958–60. (Photo: Horstheinz Neuendorff. saai.)

11,12. Egon Eiermann, design variants for a house of his own in Karlsruhe, Am Fasengarten, at the corner of Hansjakobstraße, 1958. (saai.)
13. Property Krippenhof 16/18, Baden-Baden, before the start of construction with remains of the old Krippenhof, 1958/59. (Photo: Büro Eiermann. saai.)
14. Egon Eiermann, Hardenberg Villa, Baden-Baden, 1958–60. (Photo: Horstheinz Neuendorff. saai.)

near Karlsruhe, which offered enough space for everyone. Photographs taken by the press photographer Hans Schlitz, who accompanied Eiermann for a day for an article on the »star architect« in the *Bunte Illustrierte* in 1957, show glimpses of this flat, whose living room was furnished with mass-produced furniture that Eiermann had designed for the 1949 exhibition »Wie Wohnen« (»How to Live«).[27] The all-purpose building, which could not meet the architect's demands, was considered only an interim solution from the start. In a letter, Eiermann complained about the »appalling milieu« on the faceless outskirts of the city in which he had to live there, »between American barracks, gravel pits and no-man's land«.[28] Something of his own in better surroundings was a done deal at the latest with the great success of the German Pavilion at the World's Fair in Brussels.

Initially, the focus was on a building site in the immediate vicinity of the Technische Hochschule, where an area owned by the state was reserved for the construction of professors' houses on the edge of the Fasanengarten and next to the Botanical Institute. Rudolf Büchner, an important colleague of Eiermann's from his time in Berlin and brought to the Hochschule by him as a teacher in 1952, had already built three houses for professors there.[29] Eiermann made his first plans for a still vacant corner plot in 1958. He wanted to surround the almost square plot with a high wall, and the house, for which he developed three very different approaches, was to stand in the square. One idea envisaged a two-storey residential building with a flat roof, a solitaire in the style of the Hardenberg Villa, the other a likewise two-storey, but grouped house with a gable roof, which took up the architect's older residential building designs. In the most unusual variant, two parallel, low single-storey buildings with shallowly pitched, widely overhanging roofs supported by posts were to duck into the interior, one for living, the other for sleeping – an almost monastic district secluded from the world with an additively arranged, very simple and light architecture. The pattern of the »barracks« of Beelitz-Heilstätten had obviously not yet been forgotten, and the influence of Mies van der Rohe's vitrine-like Farnsworth House and traditional Japanese houses was unmistakable. The strict separation of functions would have had far-reaching consequences for everyday life, as one would always have had to pass through the open air to get from one house to the other. The project did not go far. Eiermann had reservations about the proximity to the Hochschule. A greater physical distance from the architecture faculty, which he dominated but which also cost him an inordinate amount of energy, seemed advisable to him. His colleague Otto Ernst Schweizer had already set an example twenty years earlier with his residence in Baden-Baden. The renowned spa town, 40 km away, was in his focus in 1958 because of the Hardenberg Villa, and so the couple set out to find a suitable building site there.

The city administration under its mayor Schlapper was keen to bind the famous architect to Baden-Baden and accommodated him. He was offered a building site on the Krippenhof from municipal property, a preferred new building district with a south-west facing slope, including a view of the Oos Valley, the Kurpark opposite on the slope and the Stourdza Chapel built by Leo von Klenze. A good address in a town that has attracted spa guests from all over the world since the 19th century. The historicist Fürstenberg Monument from 1870 and the Dr. Heinsheimer Sanatorium, built in 1905 by Hermann Billing and Wilhelm Vittali, had already set architectural landmarks in the neighbourhood. The Krippenhof estate, like the adjoining manor to the east, had been parcelled out in the 1950s and developed with single-family houses and smaller two-family houses, although none of the buildings stood out for their special architectural design – »lower mediocrity«, as Eiermann stated disparagingly in a letter to the mayor.[30]

The plot in question had not previously found a buyer, presumably because it was considered difficult to build on: irregularly cut, with a considerable slope on two sides, steeper to the south, flatter to the west. The difference in height between the north-east corner and the south-west corner was more than 7 m, unfavourable for any off-the-peg house. Unusual was also the access from two sides, which had its origin in the previous development. From the southwest, the street »Krippenhof« leads to the site as a cul-de-sac street with a turning area. Before that, however, further to the southwest, an arm of the road branches off, climbs the steep slope and runs uphill along the property. The embankment wall mentioned at the beginning, as well as other wall remains from demolished buildings of the old cot yard, formed unwelcome relics on the property, which was also covered in the lower area with old chestnut trees, lime trees and ash trees that should be preserved as

sowie weitere Mauerreste von abgerissenen Baulichkeiten des alten Krippenhofs bildeten unliebsame Relikte auf dem Grundstück, das zudem im unteren Bereich mit möglichst zu schonenden alten Kastanien, Linden und Eschen bestanden war. Eiermann ließ sich von diesen Vorgaben des Ortes nicht abschrecken. Er wollte ja alles andere als ein alltägliches Haus bauen und sah die Entwurfsaufgabe hier als besondere Herausforderung an. Schon bei Häusern der Berliner Zeit hatte er es verstanden, Terrainunterschiede gestalterisch zu nutzen, etwa beim Haus für den Schauspieler und Regisseur Gustav Henckels in Klein-Machnow oder beim Haus Steingroever in Berlin-Charlottenburg.[31] Im Februar 1959 wurde Eiermann Eigentümer der 1.800 qm großen Parzelle Krippenhof 16–18, wobei er sich der Stadt gegenüber vertraglich verpflichten mußte, dort bis April 1961 einen Neubau zu errichten.[32] »Jahrelang kann man an einem Haus planen«, es sei »das größte Problem, eine Wohnstatt zu bauen«, so eine Äußerung Eiermanns. Planung und Bau des eigenen Hauses sollten bis zum Einzug gut vier Jahre in Anspruch nehmen. Es wurde, charakteristisch für den Architekten, ein langwieriger Prozeß.

Planungen

Schon 1958, noch vor dem Erwerb des Grundstücks, gab es erste Überlegungen mit zwei Varianten.[33] Beide sahen einen langgestreckten Bau mit extrem flach geneigtem Satteldach entlang des oberen Verlaufs der Straße vor. Bei beiden Alternativen sollten die tiefer, am Ende der Sackgasse mit dem Wendeplatz gelegenen Bruchsteinmauern des ehemaligen Krippenhofs weitgehend erhalten bleiben. Eine Doppelgarage sowie ein Gartenhof mit einem markanten frei stehenden Außenkamin und einer dem Haus vorgelagerten Terrasse sollten in diese Reste integriert werden. Der Neubau wäre kontrastierend dazu am Hang darüber errichtet und damit gleichsam die neue Zeit mit der ruinösen überwundenen Vergangenheit in Dialog gesetzt und die Geschichtlichkeit des Ortes betont worden. Man darf von solch einer Lösung bei Eiermann zunächst überrascht sein, dessen häufig in Lehre und öffentlichen Äußerungen wiederholtes funktionalistisches Credo es war, daß jede Generation ihr Recht habe, veraltete bauliche Zeugnisse früherer Zeiten abzureißen. In der gleichzeitig hitzig geführten öffentlichen Diskussion um seinen Wiederaufbau der Kaiser-Wilhelm-Gedächtniskirche in Berlin machte er sich vehement für den Abbruch der neoromanischen Turmruine stark. Er hatte auch keine Skrupel, sich damals dafür einzusetzen, daß eine Inkunabel der Moderne der 1920er Jahre, Erich Mendelsohns Schocken-Bau in Stuttgart, einem eigenen Warenhausneubau weichen mußte. Bei seinem Haus sah er aber offenbar einen besonderen Reiz darin, die Materialkontraste zu betonen und den bröckelnden, efeuüberwachsenen Gartenmauern in Bruchstein seinen präzisen Neubau in Beton und Backstein gegenüberzustellen. Unregelmäßiges Bruchsteinmauerwerk scheint für Eiermann generell attraktiv gewesen zu sein, erwarb er doch Ende der 1950er Jahre als Feriendomizil im Tessin ein bescheidenes »Rustico«, zwei kleine landwirtschaftliche Nebengebäude am Steilhang von Brione sopra Minusio mit grandiosem Blick auf den Lago Maggiore.[34] Er ließ den beiden primitiven Natursteinhütten ihren ursprünglichem Charme und fügte nur eine verbindende Terrasse mit Pergola im gleichen rauen Duktus hinzu – eine unerwartete Gegenwelt zu Eiermanns modernistischem Perfektionismus.

Die innere Disposition des Hauses für Baden-Baden war in Variante A und B stark bestimmt durch eine Schottenbauweise mit der Addition von sechs gleich großen Raumeinheiten, die mit Einbauschrank, Bett und Schreibplatz identisch möbliert werden sollten. Diese Einheiten sollten sich talseits gegen den Garten mit Glaswänden öffnen und an einem innenliegenden Flur reihen, der auch die Nebenräume an der weitgehend geschlossenen Straßenseite zu erschließen hatte. Zur Belichtung war hier nur ein schmales horizontales Fensterband unter der Dachtraufe vorgesehen. Ein großer gemeinschaftlicher Wohnraum hätte jenseits des Verbindungsglieds der Treppe einen seitlichen Annex gebildet, als eine Art Wohnhalle, da er unter dem gemeinsamen Dach durch seine tiefere Lage eine größere Raumhöhe erhalten hätte. Die Reihung gleicher Schotten für den Hausherrn und seine Frau, für die Tochter, die betagte Mutter Eiermann sowie einen Gast ist als Echo des eingangs zitierten Grundgedankens von Eiermann zu sehen, jedem Mitglied der Familie ein eigenes Haus im Haus zu bieten. Diese Vorstellung entsprang seiner Begeisterung für den Bautypus der Karthause, den er bei einer Urlaubsreise 1958 durch Norditalien in der Certosa di Pavia kennengelernt hatte. Wie schon Le Corbusier bei einem Besuch der Certosa San Lorenzo di Galluzzo bei Florenz 1910 sah auch Eiermann das System der historischen Karthause mit ihrer gleichförmigen Reihung von abgeschlossenen Mönchshäuschen mit jeweils eigenem Garten an einem Kreuzgang wesensverwandt mit modernem architektonischen und städtebaulichen Denken. Von Einzelhäusern unter einem Dach kann freilich bei Planung und Realisierung des Hauses Eiermann nicht die Rede sein, denn die Reihung von funktionalen Schlaf- und Arbeitszellen mit gemeinsamen Sanitärräumen jenseits des Flurs mag viel eher an ein Hotel oder Krankenhaus erinnern und bildet ein Motiv, das der Architekt schon vor 1945 bei den Kinderzimmern im Haus Vollberg und gleichzeitig auch in der Villa Hardenberg verwendet hat.

Variante A ordnet die sechs Schotten nebeneinander in einem eingeschossigen, besonders lang gestreckten Baukörper mit einem asymmetrischen Dach an. Zwei davon, jene der Eltern, sind zu einer Doppeleinheit zusammengefaßt. In den Einheiten führt jeweils eine vierstufige Treppe vom höher gelegenen Flur in die Räume hinunter. Eine breite, durchgehende Terrasse auf einer weit auskragenden, dünnen Betonplatte erscheint wie schwebend vor der gemeinsamen Glasfront über dem abschüssigen Garten und seinen ruinösen Mauern. Variante B geht von einem zweigeschossigen Bau aus, der stärker in den Hang eingetieft ist und deshalb zusätzlich mit einem Lichtgraben zur Straße ausgestattet ist. Auf der oberen Ebene reihen sich vier Raumeinheiten, auf der unteren zwei. Darüber hinaus hätte unten ein großer Eßraum und die Küche Platz gefunden, Funktionen, die bei Variante A räumlich wenig geglückt und unpraktisch für den Alltagsgebrauch offen in den schmalen Flurbereich vor den Zimmern integriert werden sollten.

Die familieninterne Diskussion um diese Entwürfe scheint intensiv gewesen sein, folgt man den Aussagen von Brigitte Eiermann. Sie betonte gerne, daß ihr Mann den Part des Planers spielte und sie, selbst Architektin, den der Bauherrin übernahm und die Benutzbarkeit reklamierte.[35] Man wurde sich aber bald einig, daß nur die Variante B, die zweigeschossige Lösung, den Aus-

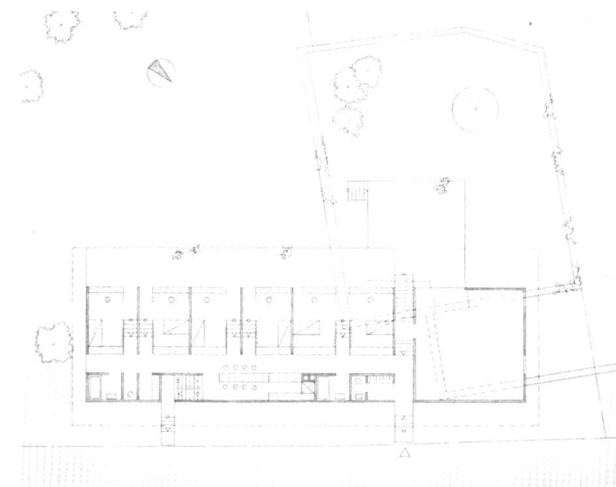

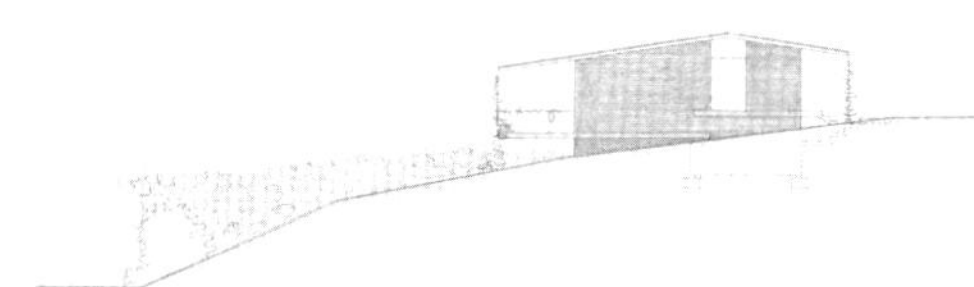

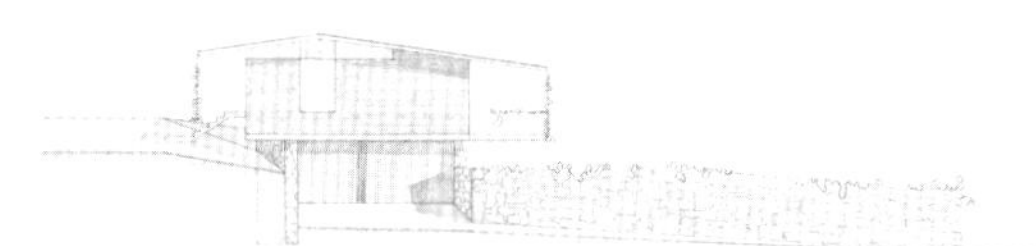

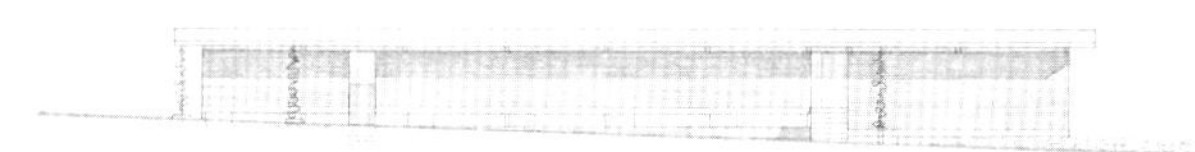

15–17. Egon Eiermann, Haus Eiermann, Baden-Baden, erster Vorentwurf, Planungsvariante A, Ende 1958, Grundriß, Aufrisse von Osten und Westen, Aufriß von Norden. (saai.)
18–20. Egon Eiermann, Haus Eiermann, Baden-Baden, erster Vorentwurf, Planungsvariante B, Ende 1958, Grundriß, Aufrisse von Osten und Westen, Aufriß von Süden. (saai.)

15–17. Egon Eiermann, Eiermann House, Baden-Baden, first preliminary draft, planning variant A, end of 1958, floor plan, elevations from the east and the west, elevation from the north. (saai.)
18–20. Egon Eiermann, Eiermann House, Baden-Baden, first preliminary draft, planning variant B, end of 1958, floor plan, elevations from the east and the west, elevation from the north. (saai

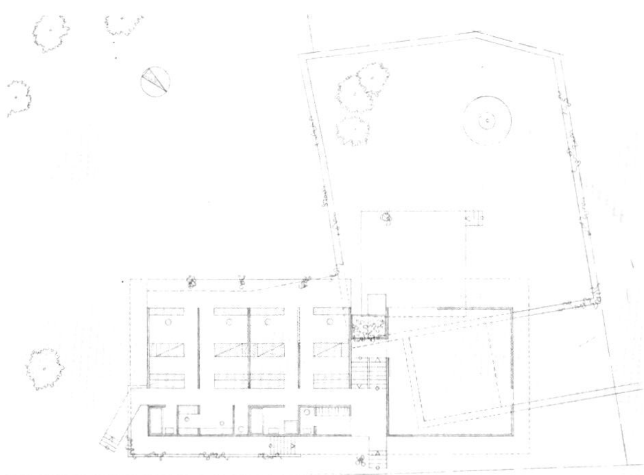

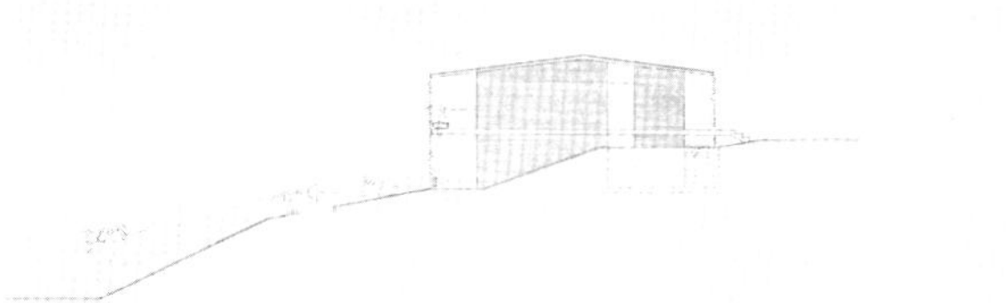

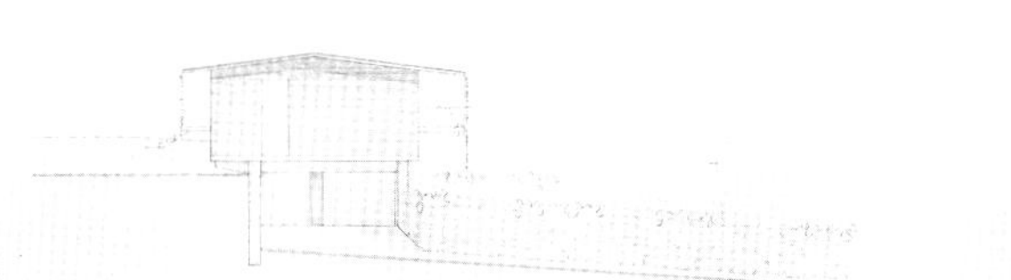

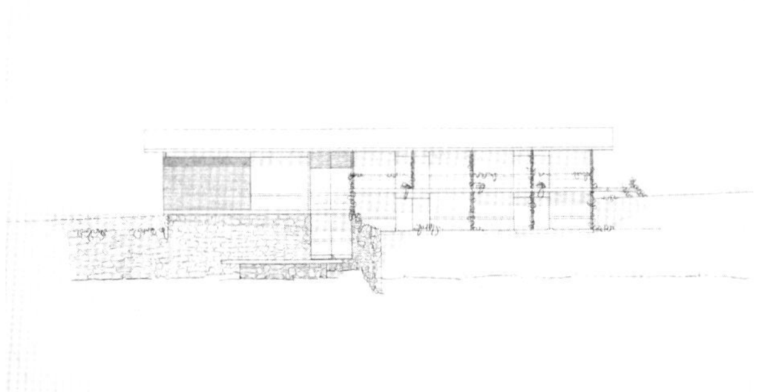

much as possible. Eiermann did not allow himself to be deterred by these specifications of the site. He wanted to build a house that was anything but everyday and saw the design task here as a special challenge. He had already understood how to use differences in terrain in the design of houses from his Berlin period, such as the house for the actor and director Gustav Henckels in Klein-Machnow or the Steingroever House in Berlin-Charlottenburg.[31] In February 1959, Eiermann became the owner of the 1,800-sqm plot Krippenhof 16–18, whereby he had to make a contractual commitment to the city to build a new house there by April 1961.[32] »You can plan on a house for years«; it is »the biggest problem to build a home«, according to one of Eiermann's statements. In fact, the planning and construction of his own house was to take a good four years until he moved in. It became, characteristically for the architect, a protracted process.

Planning

As early as 1958, even before the purchase of the property, initial considerations were made with two variants.[33] Both envisaged an elongated building with an extremely flat pitched gable roof along the upper course of the street. In both alternatives, the lower quarry stone walls of the former cot yard, located at the end of the cul-de-sac with the turning area, were to be largely preserved. A double garage as well as a garden courtyard with a prominent free-standing outdoor fireplace and a terrace in front of the house were to be integrated into these remains. The new building would have been erected in contrast on the slope above it, thus setting the new era in dialogue with the ruinous, overcome past, as it were, and emphasising the historicity of the site. One may be surprised by such a solution in Eiermann's case, whose functionalist credo, often repeated in teaching and public statements, was that every generation had its right to demolish obsolete architectural testimonies of earlier times. In the heated public debate about his reconstruction of the Kaiser Wilhelm Memorial Church in Berlin, he vehemently advocated the demolition of the neo-Romanesque tower ruins. He also had no qualms about advocating that an incunabulum of 1920s modernism, Erich Mendelsohn's Schocken building in Stuttgart, had to make way for his own new department stores. In the case of his house, however, he evidently saw a special attraction in emphasising the material contrasts and juxtaposing the crumbling, ivy-covered garden walls in quarry stone with his precise new building in concrete and brick. Irregular quarry stone masonry seems to have been attractive to Eiermann in general, as he acquired a modest »rustico«, two small agricultural ancillary buildings on the steep slope of Brione sopra Minusio with a grandiose view of Lake Maggiore, as a holiday domicile in Ticino at the end of the 1950s.[34] He left the two primitive natural stone huts their original charm and only added a connecting terrace with pergola in the same rough ductus – an unexpected counter-world to Eiermann's modernist perfectionism.

The internal disposition of the house for Baden-Baden was strongly determined in variant A and B by a bulkhead construction with the addition of six room units of equal size, which were to be furnished identically with built-in wardrobe, bed and writing desk. These units were to open up towards the garden on the valley side with glass walls and were to be lined up along an interior corridor, which was also to provide access to the adjoining rooms on the largely closed side of the street. Only a narrow horizontal band of windows under the eaves was planned for lighting. A large common living room would have formed a lateral annex beyond the connecting link of the staircase, as a kind of living hall, since its lower position would have given it greater room height under the common roof. The row of identical bulkheads for the master of the house and his wife, for the daughter, the elderly Eiermann mother and a guest can be seen as an echo of Eiermann's basic idea, quoted at the beginning, of offering each member of the family their own house within the house. This idea sprang from his enthusiasm for the Carthusian type of building, which he had become acquainted with during a holiday trip through northern Italy in 1958 in the Certosa di Pavia. Like already Le Corbusier had done on a visit to the Certosa San Lorenzo di Galluzzo near Florence in 1910, Eiermann also saw the system of the historical Carthusian monastery with its uniform row of self-contained monastic houses, each with its own garden along a cloister, as similar in essence to modern architectural and urban planning thinking. Of course, the planning and realisation of the Eiermann House cannot be said to be about individual houses under one roof, for the row of functional sleeping and working cells with common sanitary rooms beyond the corridor may be much more reminiscent of a hotel or hospital and forms a motif that the architect had already used before 1945 for the children's rooms in the Vollberg House and at the same time also in the Hardenberg Villa.

Variant A arranges the six bulkheads next to each other in a single-storey, particularly elongated structure with an asymmetrical roof. Two of them, those of the parents, are combined into a double unit. In each of the units, a four-step staircase leads down from the higher hallway to the rooms. A wide, continuous terrace on a thin, cantilevered concrete slab appears to float in front of the common glass front above the sloping garden and its ruinous walls. Variant B is based on a two-storey building that is more deeply recessed into the slope and therefore additionally equipped with a light trench to the street. Four room units would be lined up on the upper level, and two on the lower. In addition, there would have been room for a large dining room and the kitchen downstairs, functions that in variant A were spatially less successful and impractical for everyday use to be integrated openly into the hallway area in front of the rooms.

The internal family discussion about these designs seems to have been intense, according to Brigitte Eiermann. She liked to emphasise that her husband played the part of the planner and she, herself an architect, took on the part of the builder and argued for usability.[35] However, it was soon agreed that only variant B, the two-storey solution, could form the starting point for further planning. A preserved set of plans from 13 January 1959 documents that work continued on variant B. The rooms were now used as bedrooms and living quarters. The individual rooms of the family members, now designated as bedrooms and living rooms, have lost their overly strict cellular character with a wider floor plan and in the furnishing. The common living space has also become larger. Instead of a square floor plan, it now has a rectangular layout extended along the longitudinal axis of the house. The layout with a double flight of stairs at the entrance to the house on the street – one flight leads

gangspunkt für die weitere Planung bilden konnte. Ein erhaltener Plansatz vom 13. Januar 1959 dokumentiert, daß an der Variante B weitergearbeitet wurde. Die nun als Schlaf- und Wohnräume bezeichneten Einzelzimmer der Familienmitglieder haben mit einem breiteren Grundriß und in der Möblierung den allzu strengen Zellencharakter verloren. Auch der gemeinsame Wohnraum ist größer geworden. Er bekam anstelle eines quadratischen Grundrisses nun einen in der Längsachse des Hauses verlängerten rechteckigen Zuschnitt. Die Anlage mit doppelläufiger Treppe am Hauseingang an der Straße – ein Lauf führt im Freien hinauf ins obere Geschoß, einer hinab ins untere – sowie ebenfalls doppelläufiger Treppe im Inneren, die auf komplexe Weise die gegenseitig versetzten Stockwerke des Zimmertrakts mit dem Wohnraum verbindet, nähert sich bereits der realisierten Form an. Die Erhaltung der alten Mauern des Krippenhofs wurde zu diesem Zeitpunkt noch beibehalten.

Das sollte sich in einer weiteren Planstufe bis zum Sommer 1959 ändern. Der persönliche Raumbedarf des Bauherrn stieg. Sein eigener Wohn- und Schlafraum, gleich groß mit denen der anderen Familienmitglieder, reichte nicht auch noch zum Arbeiten. Die Lösung lag in der Planung jenes zweiten, kleineren Hauses, quergestellt zum Haupthaus auf dem tiefergelegenen Niveau der Sackgasse mit dem Wendeplatz. Es sollte nun die Doppelgarage aufnehmen und im Obergeschoß einen großen Atelierraum, der sich in entgegengesetzter Richtung zum höhergelegenen terrassierten Garten öffnet. Eine Außentreppe sollte seitlich von der Straße hinauf in den Garten führen, und gleichzeitig das Nebenhaus mit eigenem Eingang erschließen. Eiermann wollte für sich ein separates Refugium, in das er sich zurückziehen konnte. Dem Karthäuserideal des »Hauses im Haus« kam er damit – wenn auch nicht für die anderen Familienmitglieder – so doch für seine Person noch nahe. Die Reste des Krippenhofs mußten bei diesem Projekt, das stärker in die Topographie eingriff, freilich weitgehend aufgegeben werden, wobei zunächst noch mehr alte Mauern in den Garten integriert werden sollten als die große Böschungsmauer, die am Ende übrigblieb. Am Haupthaus selbst trat anstelle der bislang vorgesehenen Garage unter dem Wohnraum eine offene Gartenloggia.

Mit dieser baulichen Anordnung hatte das Projekt eine Form gefunden, mit der Eiermann grundsätzlich zufrieden war. Im August 1959 reichte er diese Planung zur Genehmigung beim Baden-Badener Bauordnungsamt ein, durchaus im Bewußtsein, daß noch zahlreiche weitere Entwurfsstufen und Nachtragsgesuche erforderlich sein könnten, bis der Bau seine definitive Form gefunden haben würde. Die Behörde tat sich nicht leicht mit dem Projekt, das sich dem Gewohnten entzog. Es wurde gut zwei Monate später zwar grundsätzlich genehmigt, und Eiermann erhielt auch eine Ausnahmegenehmigung für die nur 15 Grad geneigten Dächer, welche die für den Bereich am Krippenhof im Bebauungsplan vorgeschriebenen 30 bis 35 Grad deutlich unterschritten. Aber die vorgesehenen Faserzement-Wellplatten als Dachdeckung war den Baubeamten ein Dorn im Auge. Als entgegenkommender Kompromiß wurde ein Anstrich der Faserzementplatten »im Ton dunkel engobierter Ziegel oder im Schieferton« zur Auflage gemacht – woran sich Eiermann natürlich nicht zu halten gedachte.[36]

Doch zunächst drückten den Architekten andere Probleme. Unvorhergesehene Schwierigkeiten bremsten den Fortschritt des Projekts. Das Büro stellte fest, daß die amtliche Vermessung des Terrains einen Fehler aufwies. Man war deshalb bisher im Büro von falschen Maßen ausgegangen. Der Niveauunterschied von der Straße unten am Wendeplatz bis zur Straße oben erwies sich um 1,20 m höher als angegeben. Das Verhältnis der beiden Häuser zueinander stimmte deshalb nicht wie im Bauantrag dargestellt. Es mußte umgeplant werden. Gleichzeitig war das Büro Eiermann durch verschiedene große Bauprojekte für das Versandunternehmen Neckermann in Frankfurt, die Warenhäuser Horten in Stuttgart und Heidelberg, die Villa Hardenberg in Baden-Baden sowie vor allem den Wiederaufbau der Kaiser-Wilhelm-Gedächtniskirche in Berlin stark ausgelastet. Zudem stand es um die persönlichen Finanzen des Architekten um 1960 nicht zum besten. Allzu bereitwillig hatte Eiermann den eigenen Geldbeutel geöffnet, wenn es darum ging, seine ambitionierten gestalterischen Vorstellungen durchzusetzen. So trug er selbst die Kosten für den von ihm eigenmächtig entschiedenen Standortwechsel des neuen Turms der Gedächtniskirche und bezahlte das erforderlich werdende neue Fundament, obwohl das erste schon fertiggestellt war. Die Mehrkosten der Einzelbestuhlung der Kirche, die er anstelle der von der Gemeinde für ausreichend gehaltenen Möblierung mit viel günstigeren Bänken unbedingt realisieren wollte, gingen auch zu seinen Lasten. Und Eiermanns Manie, Gestaltungsvarianten an einer Vielzahl von teuren Architekturmodellen prüfen zu wollen, erwies sich gerade bei der Gedächtniskirche als pekuniäres Desaster, da er auch diese selbst zu bezahlen hatte. Der eigene Hausbau mußte wohl oder übel für eine gewisse Zeit zurückstehen, zumal sich auch mit dem Tod der Mutter Eiermanns der familiäre Hintergrund änderte. Gravierender noch war in diesen schwierigen Jahren um 1960 der Gesundheitszustand des Architekten. Im August 1960 erlitt Eiermann, aufgerieben vom leidenschaftlichen wie selbstzerstörerischen Engagement in Berlin, einen Herzinfarkt, der ihn über Monate zu Krankenhaus- und Sanatoriumsaufenthalten zwang. Auf Antrag bei der Stadt Baden-Baden wurde die im Kaufvertrag festgelegte Frist zur Fertigstellung des Hauses wegen der besonderen persönlichen Umstände bis Februar 1962 verlängert, wobei auch dieses Datum nicht eingehalten werden konnte.

Erst rund ein Jahr nach der ersten Baugenehmigung kam Ende 1960 wieder Bewegung in die Planung. Eiermann befand sich noch in einer Kurklinik am Tegernsee. Er scheint selbst von dort eine Fülle von schnell hingeworfenen Skizzen ins Büro geschickt zu haben, die von den Büromitarbeitern Rudolf Wiest und Abdullah Brechna, die für die Entwurfsplanung des Hauses zuständig waren, in Reinzeichnungen umgesetzt wurden. Beide reisten eigens nach Bayern, um diese mit dem Chef zu besprechen. Der zeigte sich nach dem Besuch befriedigt über die Weiterentwicklung, vor allem was den Wegfall des Lichtgrabens auf der Straßenseite des großen Hauses und die Lösung mit dem Nebeneingang und einem nicht einsehbaren Wäschetrockenplatz an der Schmalseite dieses Bauteils anging. Außerdem zeichnete sich ab, daß das kleine Haus nun sogar dreigeschossig werden sollte, über der nur 2 m hohen Garage ein Geschoß für das Atelier sowie darüber noch ein Emporen- oder sogar Vollgeschoß für sein persönliches Wohnen. Grundsätzliche Dinge, wie die Frage nach dem Baumaterial, blieben aber immer noch offen. Eiermann sympathisierte mit einer Konstruktion in Teakholz, wie er sie 1959 zeitweilig auch gerne bei der Wabenfassade der Gedächtniskirche gesehen hätte. Wie existenziell

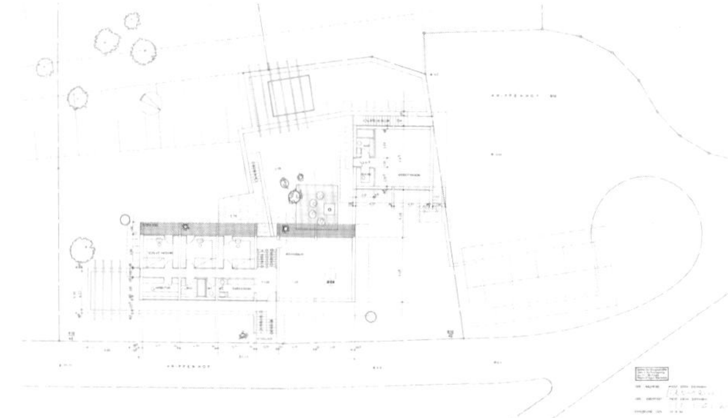

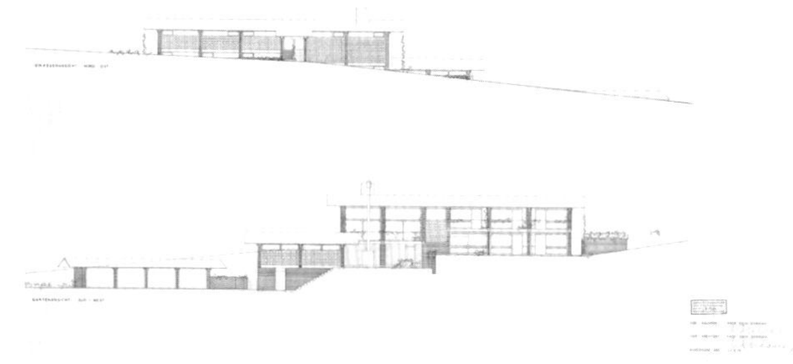

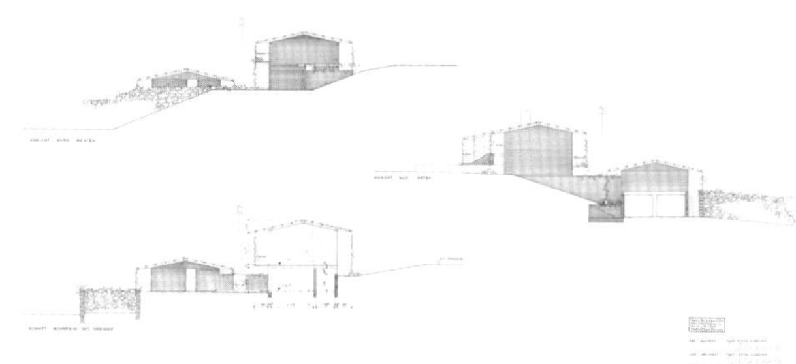

21–23. Egon Eiermann, Haus Eiermann, Baden-Baden, erste Genehmigungsplanung mit zweigeschossigem Atelierbau, August 1959, Grundriß, Aufrisse von Norden und Süden, Aufrisse von Westen und Osten. (saai.)
24–26. Egon Eiermann, Haus Eiermann, Baden-Baden, Entwurfsskizzen Eiermanns mit dreigeschossigem Atelierhaus, Ende 1960, Aufriß von Süden, Aufriß von Westen, Grundriß. (saai.)
27, 28. Veränderter Entwurf mit dreigeschossigem Atelierhaus, Anfang 1961, Aufrisse von Westen und Osten. (saai.)

21–23. Egon Eiermann, Eiermann House, Baden-Baden, first approval planning with two-storey studio building, August 1959, floor plan, elevations from the north and the south, elevations from the west and the east. (saai.)
24–26. Egon Eiermann, Eiermann House, Baden-Baden, design sketches by Eiermann with three-storey studio building, late 1960, elevation from the south, elevation from the west, floor plan. (saai.)
27, 28. Egon Eiermann, Eiermann House, Baden-Baden, modified design with three-storey studio building, early 1961, elevations from the west and the east. (saai.)

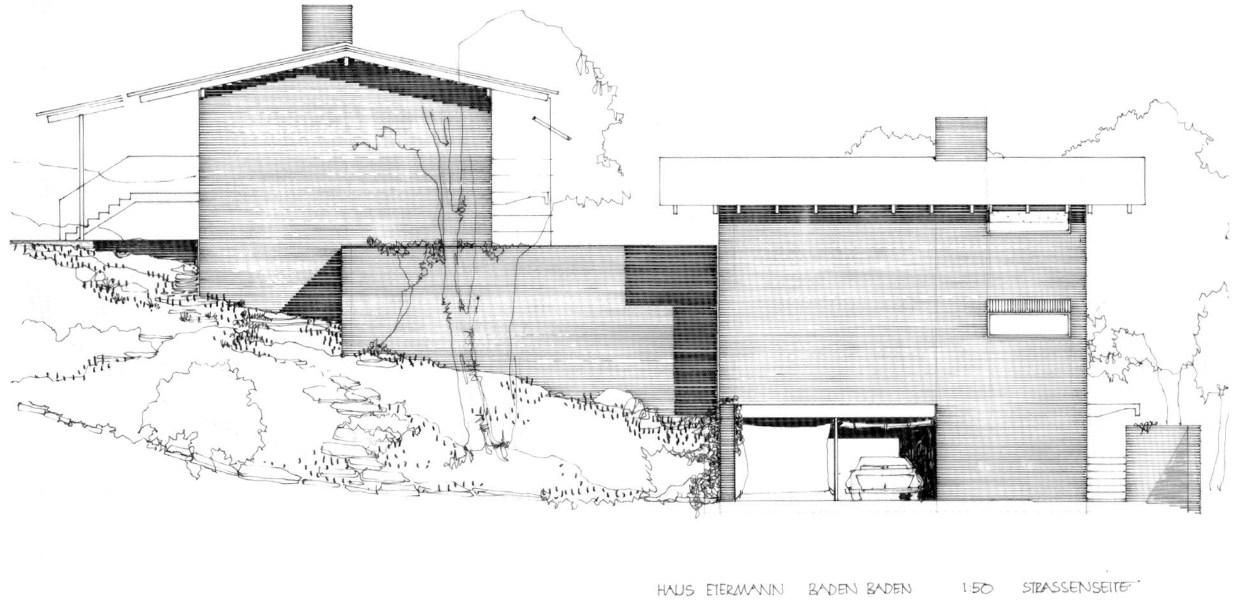

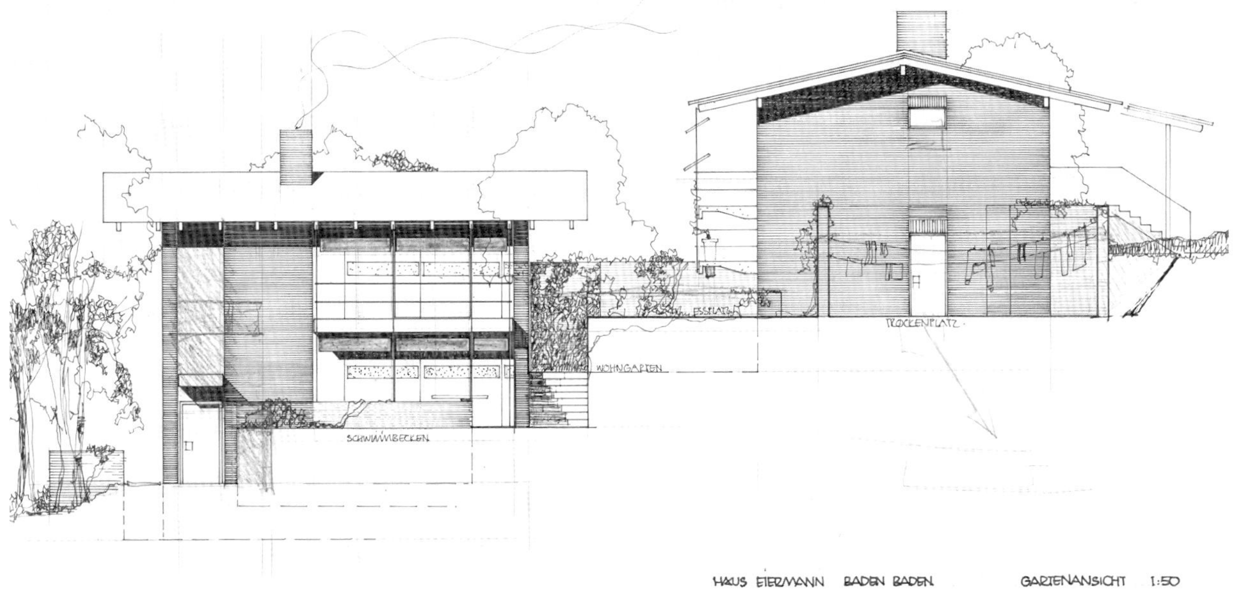

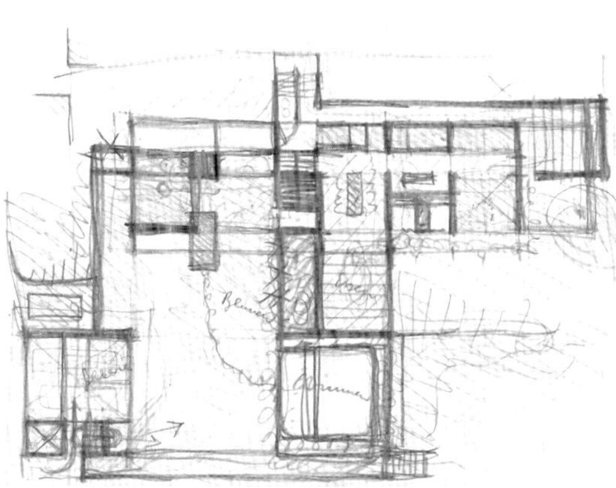

outside up to the upper floor, one down to the lower floor – as well as a double flight of stairs inside, which connects the mutually offset floors of the room wing with the living space in a complex way, already approximates the realised form. The preservation of the old walls of the cot courtyard was still maintained at this stage.

This was to change in a further planning stage up to the summer of 1959. The owner's personal space requirements increased. His own living room and bedroom, the same size as those of the other family members, were not enough for him to work in. The solution was to plan a second, smaller building, at right angles to the main building on the lower level of the cul-de-sac with the turning area. It was to house the double garage and a large studio on the upper floor, which would open in the opposite direction to the terraced garden on the higher level. An external staircase was to lead up from the street to the garden, and at the same time open up the adjoining building with its own entrance. Eiermann wanted a separate refuge for himself to which he could withdraw. He thus came close to the Carthusian ideal of the »house within a house« – if not for the other family members, then at least for himself. The remains of the cot courtyard had to be largely abandoned for this project, which intervened more strongly in the topography, whereby initially even more old walls were to be integrated into the garden than the large embankment wall that remained in the end. On the main building itself, an open garden loggia took the place of the previously planned garage under the living space.

With this structural arrangement, the project had found a form with which Eiermann was basically satisfied. In August 1959, he submitted this plan to the Baden-Baden building regulations office for approval, well aware that numerous further design stages and supplementary applications might be necessary until the building had found its definitive form. The authorities did not take it easy with the project, which defied the usual. It was approved in principle a good two months later, and Eiermann also received an exemption for the roof slope of only 15 degrees, which was well below the 30 to 35 degrees prescribed for the area at Krippenhof in the de-

ihm das eigene Haus gerade in seiner als unerträglich empfundenen gesundheitlichen Lage erschien, zeigt eine schriftliche Aufforderung aus der Klinik an Wiest und Brechna in Karlsruhe: »Ich bitte Euch mit aller Herzlichkeit: nehmt Euch dieses Hauses so an, daß wir bald zum Bauen kommen. Mein ganzes Glück hängt daran.«[37]

Im Januar 1961 erwähnte Eiermann, wieder nach Karlsruhe zurückgekehrt, dem Bauordnungsamt gegenüber erstmals, daß er wegen der neuen Höhenmessungen nun planen würde, das kleine Haus dreigeschossig zu bauen, damit der architektonische und räumliche Zusammenhang mit dem oberen Haus gewahrt bliebe. Diese Absicht sprach sich im Krippenhof schnell herum und stieß auf heftige Kritik. Vor allem der einflußreiche unmittelbare Nachbar, Leiter des Sparkassen- und Giroverbandes in Baden, meldete vehementen Widerspruch an. Er unterstellte zu Unrecht, daß der Architekt sein Karlsruher Büro mit 25 bis 30 Mitarbeitern in den immer größer werdenden Annex verlegen wolle und befürchtete dadurch eine unzumutbare Lärmbelästigung. Erst nachdem Eiermann, sichtlich ungehalten über den Gegenwind, sich schriftlich verpflichtete, den Bau niemals gewerblich zu nutzen, war den Opponenten der Wind aus den Segeln genommen.

Im Lauf des Jahres 1961 kristallisierte sich allmählich die Form der Entwurfsplanung heraus, nach der das Haus schließlich gebaut wurde. Wie bei den Vorplanungen war es eine allmähliche Genese. Auf die Schnelle gefundene Lösungen waren nicht Eiermanns Sache. Er versuchte, ständig in Varianten zu denken und diese laufend zu verbessern. Permanent lieferte er dem Büro neue Skizzen zur Weiterbearbeitung. Daneben betrieb er auch persönlich einen intensiven Briefwechsel mit Behörden, Sachverständigen und Firmen. Eine Zwischenstufe des Entwurfs, von Abdullah Brechna gezeichnet und auf Anfang 1961 zu datieren, zeigt die später realisierte Gebäudegruppe schon in den wesentlichen Grundzügen. Wichtige Einzelheiten des ausgeführten Baues, beispielsweise die Fensteröffnungen des Atelierhauses zur Straße hin, sollten sich noch ändern, die Außentreppe vom Wendeplatz des Krippenhofs hinauf in den Garten noch eine andere Lage und Form bekommen. Andere Elemente wie ein zunächst geplantes Schwimmbecken vor der Gartenfront des Atelierhauses sollten ganz wegfallen und beispielsweise durch ein kleines Tauchbecken mit Dusche ersetzt werden, das im unteren Garten einen wichtigen Kontrapunkt zur Hausgruppe bilden wird.

Im Juli 1961 wurde der Nachtrag zum Baugesuch mit dem dreigeschossigen Atelierhaus genehmigt. Wiederum war die Stadt Eiermann entgegengekommen, denn eigentlich waren drei Vollgeschosse im Neubaugebiet des Krippenhofs nicht konform mit dem Bebauungsplan. Die endgültigen Pläne waren im November fertig. Die abschließende Baugenehmigung erfolgte sogar erst im Februar 1962.

Die Bauausführung

Im Sommer 1961 konnte unberührt davon schon mit den Bauarbeiten begonnen werden. Sie schritten zunächst zügig voran. Dies war vor allem der Verdienst des Architekten Kurt Huppert, der im Büro seit dem Vorjahr an der Planung mitwirkte und den Eiermann nun zum Bauleiter in Baden-Baden machte.[38] Ihm oblag nicht nur die Organisation der Baustelle, sondern auch die Werkplanung für den inneren Ausbau – jenes Finish, auf den Eiermann größten Wert legte, da für ihn die Qualität jedes einzelnen Details, wie schon eingangs zitiert, das eigentlich Noble in der Architektur ausmachte. Eiermann stand damit im Gegensatz zu dem rationalen Funktionalismus, den er gern in Worten propagierte, während er in seinem Schaffen noch ganz in der Tradition der Vorstellungen vom Gesamtkunstwerk des anbrechenden 20. Jahrhunderts stand, die ihm von seinem Lehrer Hans Poelzig vermittelt worden waren. Viele Dutzend im Eiermann-Nachlaß erhaltene Skizzen für Detaillösungen sowie Notizzettel mit Aufforderungen und Wünschen des Architekten an seinen Mitarbeiter Huppert dokumentieren die enge Kommunikation bei allen im weiteren Bauverlauf anfallenden Fragen. Und Huppert hatte die besondere Fähigkeit, die Intentionen seines Chefs zu dessen voller Zufriedenheit umzusetzen.

Haustechnik

Bauphotos überliefern den großen Umfang der notwendigen Erdarbeiten am Hang nach dem Abbruch der Krippenhof-Reste. Im Chaos der Baustelle zeichnet sich indes schon die für Eiermann charakteristische Perfektion des Rohbaus ab. Die Terrassen, die schottenartigen Querwände und geschlossenen Außenwände wurden über Betonfundamenten massiv in Backstein gemauert. Dank der ausgefeilten Planung mußte kein einziger sichtbarer Backstein geteilt werden, für Eiermann ein Grundsatz jeglicher Gestaltqualität beim Bauen, den er auch seinen Studenten einbläute, von denen er schon im Grundstudium das akribische Zeichnen von Fliesen- und Mauerwerksplänen verlangte. In Mauern und Betondecken wurden bereits Leerrohre für die gesamte Installation verlegt, was ebenfalls eine immense und exakte planerische Vorarbeit nötig machte. Überhaupt wurde der Haustechnik und deren individueller, nicht nur technisch, sondern auch formal befriedigender Lösung größte Bedeutung beigemessen. Die Hauptstränge der Elektroleitungen wurden im Hohlraum des doppelschaligen Daches zugänglich verlegt. Selbst die Sicherungstafel im Keller unter dem großen Wohnraum besitzt ästhetische Qualitäten. Die Hausklingel wird nicht über einen Knopf an der Wand neben der Eingangstür bedient, sondern über eine am Kabel vom Vordach herunterhängende Vorrichtung wie der Notrufknopf an einem Krankenbett, den Eiermann bei seinem langen Krankenhausaufenthalt kurz zuvor schätzen gelernt haben dürfte. Beide Hausteile erhielten eine mit Warmwasser betriebene Fußbodenheizung, bei Bedarf konnten Infrarotstrahler in den Wohn- und Schlafräumen als weitere Wärmequelle zugeschaltet werden. Die Strahler durchziehen die Wohn- und Schlafräume in den abgehängten Holzdecken als linienförmiges Gestaltungselement. Ihr technischer Charakter mit Heizstab und verchromten Reflektoren ist in Kontrast zum natürlichen Holz gesetzt und dient nicht nur einfach als Wärmequelle, sondern ist bewußt auch zur Gliederung des Raumes eingesetzt. Die Beleuchtung wird in Betrieb genommen mittels Zugschaltern, Hanfseilen mit eigens gedrechselten runden Holzgriffen in Oregon Pine, die von der Decke herunterhängen. Mit einer Klingelanlage, gestaltet mit runden Plexiglasscheiben an der Wand, kann man sich von jedem Zimmer aus in der Küche bemerkbar machen, ein erstaunliches Nachleben jener Glockenzüge in vornehmen Villenhaushalten

29, 30. Die Baustelle des Hauses Eiermann, Baden-Baden, 1961. (saai.)

29, 30. The construction site of the Eiermann House, Baden-Baden, 1961. (saai.)

velopment plan. But the planned fibre-cement roofing was a thorn in the side of the building officials. As an accommodating compromise, they stipulated that the fibre-cement panels be painted »in the shade of dark engobed tiles or in the shade of slate« – which Eiermann, of course, did not intend to adhere to.[36]

But at first, other problems pressed the architect. Unforeseen difficulties slowed down the progress of the project. The office discovered that there was a mistake in the official survey of the terrain. Therefore, the office had assumed that the measurements were wrong. The difference in level from the road below at the turning area to the road above turned out to be 1.20 m higher than indicated. The relationship of the two houses to each other was therefore not as shown in the planning application. It had to be redesigned. At the same time, Eiermann's office was very busy with various large construction projects for the mail-order company Neckermann in Frankfurt, the Horten department stores in Stuttgart and Heidelberg, the Hardenberg Villa in Baden-Baden and, above all, the reconstruction of the Kaiser Wilhelm Memorial Church in Berlin. In addition, the architect's personal finances were not at their best around 1960. Eiermann was all too willing to open his own purse when it came to implementing his ambitious design ideas. For example, he himself bore the costs for the change of location of the new tower of the Memorial Church, which he decided on his own authority, and paid for the new foundation that became necessary, even though the first one had already been completed. The additional costs of the individual seating in the church, which he insisted on realising with much cheaper benches instead of the furniture that the congregation considered sufficient, were also at his expense. And Eiermann's mania for testing design variants on a multitude of expensive architectural models proved to be a pecuniary disaster, especially with the Gedächtniskirche, since he had to pay for it himself. The construction of his own house had to take a back seat for a while, if need be, especially since Eiermann's family background changed with the death of his mother. Even more serious in these difficult years around 1960 was the architect's state of health. In August 1960, Eiermann, worn down by his passionate and self-destructive commitment in Berlin, suffered a heart attack that forced him to spend months in hospital and a sanatorium. On application to the city of Baden-Baden, the deadline for completion of the house stipulated in the purchase contract was extended until February 1962 due to the special personal circumstances, although even this date could not be met.

It was not until about a year after the first building permit was granted that the plans began to move again at the end of 1960. Eiermann was still in a spa clinic at Tegernsee. It seems that he himself sent a wealth of sketches from there to the office, which were then converted into final drawings by the office staff Rudolf Wiest and Abdullah Brechna, who were responsible for the design planning of the house. Both travelled to Bavaria especially to discuss them with the boss. After the visit, the boss was satisfied with the further development, especially with regard to the omission of the light trench on the street side of the large building and the solution with the side entrance and a laundry drying area on the narrow side of this part of the building that cannot be seen. In addition, it became apparent that the side building would now even have three storeys, with a storey for the studio above the garage, which was only 2 m high, and a gallery or even a full storey for his personal living quarters. Fundamental matters, however, such as the question of the building material, still remained open. Eiermann sympathised with a construction in teak, as he would have liked to see for a time in 1959 in the honeycomb façade of the Gedächtniskirche. A written request from the clinic to Wiest and Brechna in Karlsruhe shows how existential his own house seemed to him, especially in his health situation, which he found unbearable: »I ask you with all my heart: take care of this house in such a way that we can soon start building. My whole happiness hangs on it.«[37]

In January 1961, when Eiermann returned to Karlsruhe, he mentioned for the first time to the building regulations office that, because of the new height measurements, he was now planning to build the side building three storeys high, so that the architectural and spatial connection with the upper building would be preserved. Word of this intention spread quickly in the Krippenhof and was met with fierce criticism. Above all, the influential immediate neighbour, head of the Savings Banks and Giro Association in Baden, voiced vehement opposition. He wrongly insinuated that the architect wanted to move his Karlsruhe office with 25 to 30 employees to the ever-growing annex and feared that this would cause unacceptable noise pollution. Only after Eiermann, visibly displeased by the headwind, committed himself in writing never to use the building for commercial purposes, was the wind taken out of the opponents' sails.

In the course of 1961, the form of the design planning gradually crystallised according to which the house was finally built. As with the preliminary planning, it was a gradual genesis. Solutions found in a hurry were not Eiermann's thing. He tried to think constantly in terms of variants and to improve them continuously. He constantly provided the office with new sketches for further work. In addition, he also personally engaged in intensive correspondence with authorities, experts and companies. An intermediate stage of the design, drawn by Abdullah Brechna and dated early 1961, already shows the essential features of the building group that was later realised. Important details of the completed building, for example the window openings of the studio building facing the street, were still to be changed, and the external staircase from the turning area of the Krippenhof up to the garden was to be given a different position and form. Other elements, such as an initially planned swimming pool in front of the garden front of the studio building, were to be omitted altogether and replaced, for example, by a small plunge pool with shower, which will form an important counterpoint to the group of houses in the lower garden.

In July 1961, the addendum to the building application with the three-storey building was approved. Again the city had accommodated Eiermann, although actually three full storeys in the new building area of the Krippenhof were not in conformity with the development plan. The final plans were ready in November. The final building permit was not even issued until February 1962.

The construction work

In the summer of 1961, construction work could begin without being affected by this. At first they progressed rapidly. This was mainly thanks to the architect Kurt

der Kaiserzeit, an die sich Eiermann noch aus seiner Jugend in Babelsberg erinnert haben dürfte. Für heiße Sommertage hatte sich Eiermann zudem eine sehr ungewöhnliche Berieselungsanlage zur Kühlung einfallen lassen. Ein frei über der Gartenseite des Daches im großen Haus verlaufendes perforiertes Wasserrohr spendete bei Bedarf Wasser auf die Faserzement-Wellplatten.[39] Das Wasser kühlte aber nicht nur, es bot beim Abfließen über die weit vorstehende Traufe zugleich ein faszinierendes Schauspiel mit einem glitzernden Vorhang herabfallender Tropfen.

Fassaden

Im Gegensatz zur Geschlossenheit des massiven Mauerwerks der Giebelwände und der Straßenfassade des Haupthauses steht die weitgehende Auflösung der Gartenfassaden. Dies geschieht nicht nur mittels raumhoher und raumbreiter Glasflächen in ihren von außen bündig mit der Fassade abschließenden Naturholzrahmen, sondern auch durch eine gerüsthaft räumliche Zwischenzone zwischen innen und außen, die den Fronten vorgelegt ist. Leichte, profilierte Betonkragplatten in Bodenhöhe und dünnes, weiß lackiertes Metallgestänge, daran schräg gestellt mit Hanfseilen befestigter takelageartiger Sonnenschutz aus naturfarbenem Segeltuch sowie das extrem überstehende, von schmalen Holzsparren getragene Dach aus Faserzement-Wellplatten mit ornamentalhafter Wellenkante heben die Schwere des Baukörpers optisch auf.

Eiermann hatte die Umgangsfassade mit Metallgestänge und integriertem Sonnenschutz erstmals 1953 beim Bau des Warenhauses Merkur in Reutlingen entwickelt, um das Reinigen der Fenster, das beim wenig früheren Merkur-Haus in Heilbronn nur unter großem Aufwand möglich war, zu erleichtern. Nachdem sich auch die besondere ästhetische Qualität der gerüstartigen Konstruktion offenbart hatte, kultivierte Eiermann diese Lösung variierend von Projekt zu Projekt. Spätestens mit dem Deutschen Pavillon auf der Weltausstellung in Brüssel war das Motiv zu einem Markenzeichen seines Schaffens geworden. Bei der 1961 fertiggestellten Zentrale des Versandunternehmens Neckermann in Frankfurt wurden statt beweglicher Jalousien erstmals fest stehende und schräg gestellte Sonnensegel in das Gestänge integriert. Diese Form sollte Eiermann im gesamten Spätwerk bis hin zu den erst posthum fertiggestellten Olivetti-Türmen in Frankfurt immer wieder verwenden. Es war sein wichtigster Beitrag zur zeitgenössischen Architektur. Sein Typus der Umgangsfassade wurde in den 1960er- und frühen 1970er Jahren international rezipiert, allerdings selten in der für Eiermann charakteristischen Feingliedrigkeit. Auch bei seinem eigenen Haus legte er großen Wert auf die Details dieser diaphanen Struktur und war bestrebt, deren Gestaltung besonders filigran zu halten. Den Statiker, der die ungenügende Belastbarkeit der Konstruktion bemängelte und die Baubehörde darauf aufmerksam machte, daß eine Nutzlast von 100 kg/qm für die Balkone zu berechnen sei, diese somit deutlich massiver ausfallen müßten, traf der heftige Zorn Eiermanns. In einem seiner berüchtigten Briefe rechnete er mit ihm ab, bezichtigte ihn bürokratischer Sturheit und warf ihm vor, eine wirklichkeitsfremde Paragraphenreiterei zu betreiben.[40] Er nahm die Sache in der Folge selbst in die Hand und erreichte eine Ausnahmegenehmigung, indem er die Funktion als Balkon bestritt und die Auskragungen vor den Fenstern als Blumenborde deklarierte. Dabei war das Hinaustreten auf den schmalen Steg vor den Fenstern durchaus beabsichtigt, nicht nur für die Glasreinigung. Aber es waren eben tatsächlich auch Blumenborde, denn die dekorative Reihung kreisrunder Aussparungen in den Kragplatten sollte von Anfang an handelsübliche Tontöpfe aufnehmen, bepflanzt mit Sommerblumen. Meist war es wuchernde Kapuzinerkresse mit üppig herunterhängenden Ranken. Damit nahm Eiermann eine alte ländliche Tradition auf, vor Stubenfenstern in Bauernhäusern Bretter mit ausgesägten Löchern anzubringen, in die im Sommer Blumentöpfe eingestellt werden konnten, wobei überschüssiges Gießwasser durch das Loch im Topfboden frei nach unten abtropfen konnte. Und er führte zudem ein Motiv des Landhausbaus vom Anfang seines Jahrhunderts weiter, wo Blumenborde vor den Fenstern eine wichtige Rolle als Gestaltungselement spielten, etwa bei den Bauten von Josef Maria Olbrich auf der Darmstädter Mathildenhöhe.

Garten

Haus und Garten bildeten für Eiermann eine gestalterische wie ideelle Einheit. Auch dies war Teil einer bürgerlichen Baukultur, die er in der Umgebung seiner Jugend vor dem Ersten Weltkrieg in Babelsberg kennengelernt hatte. Zur Planung der Gärten seiner Berliner Vorkriegshäuser, etwa dem Haus Vollberg, zog er mehrfach die damals noch junge Gartenarchitektin Herta Hammerbacher heran, ausgebildet in der Bornimer Schule Karl Foersters im nahen Potsdam. Ihre Arbeiten zeigen eine naturnahe, standortgemäße Bepflanzung mit Büschen, Stauden und Gräsern, ähnlich den Gärten von Eiermanns frühen Häusern, bei denen sich kein professioneller Gartenplaner nachweisen läßt. Auffällig ist jeglicher Verzicht auf formale Elemente wie geschnittene Hecken oder geometrische und farbige Blumenbeete, wie sie in den 1920er Jahren in Gärten Usus waren. Das große Umfeld der Villa Hardenberg ließ er im Einvernehmen mit der Bauherrin nach eigenen Angaben zurückhaltend gestalten. Es kam ihm vor allem darauf an, das Gebäude mit seinem von Knöterich überwachsenen Gestänge freigestellt auf Rasenflächen zu präsentieren und Grundstücksgrenzen möglichst dicht mit Büschen zuzupflanzen, um Einblicke zu verhindern und ungeliebte Nachbarbauten verschwinden zu lassen. Auch dort waren Blumenbeete nicht gefragt.

Bei den Überlegungen für das eigene Haus wandte er sich bereits im Frühjahr 1961 an den Gartenarchitekten Toni Jelinek in Frankfurt. Dessen Gartengestaltung des Hauses Feith im dortigen Villenviertel Lerchesberg, zu dem Eiermann Pläne beigesteuert hatte, war ihm als »klug und hübsch« aufgefallen.[41] Bei Jelinek erhoffte er sich ein räumliches Verständnis, das, wie er ihm schrieb, seiner Meinung nach vielen Gartenarchitekten fehle. Als im Juni 1962 die Bauarbeiten entsprechend weit gediehen waren, schickte er Jelinek einen Grundstücksplan, in den er seine gemeinsam mit Brigitte Eiermann entwickelten Vorstellungen grob eingezeichnet hatte. Früheren Ideen von Jelinek erteilte er »als komische Vorschläge […] mit Taxus und ähnlichen scheußlichen Friedhofsdingen« eine Abfuhr. Er wolle alles andere haben als einen schicken Garten, »keine Anlage, wie Sie sie vielleicht durch Ihre Frankfurter Kundschaft gewöhnt sind, sondern eine natürliche und eher wilde als gezähmte Sa-

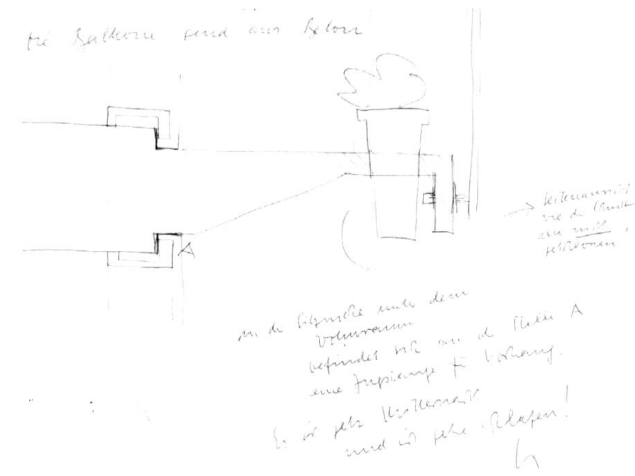

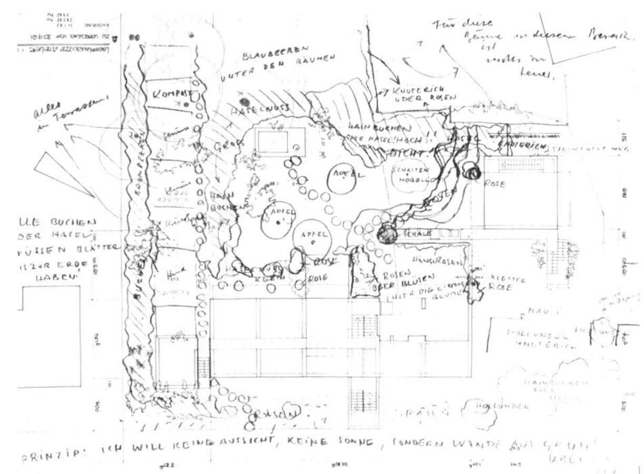

31. Egon Eiermann, Haus Eiermann, Baden-Baden, Skizze von Eiermann für das Profil der Balkone vor den Fenstern, 1961. (saai.)
32. Egon Eiermann, Haus Eiermann, Baden-Baden, Skizze von Eiermann zur Bepflanzung des Gartens, 1961. (saai.)
33. Egon Eiermann, Warenhaus Merkur, Reutlingen, 1952/53, erstes Beispiel im Werk Eiermanns mit umlaufenden Umgängen und Jalousien als Sonnenschutz. (Photo: Walter Hennenlotter. saai.)
34. Egon Eiermann, Versandhaus Neckermann, Frankfurt am Main, 1958–1961, mit umlaufenden Umgängen und schräggestelltem Sonnenschutz in Textilbespannung. (Photo: Horstheinz Neuendorff. saai.)

31. Egon Eiermann, Eiermann House, Baden-Baden, sketch by Eiermann for the profile of the balconies in front of the windows, 1961. (saai.)
32. Egon Eiermann, Eiermann House, Baden-Baden, sketch for the planting of the garden, 1961. (saai.)
33. Egon Eiermann, Merkur department store, Reutlingen, 1952/53, first example in Eiermann's œuvre of circumferential walkways and blinds as sun protection. (Photo: Walter Hennenlotter. saai.)
34. Egon Eiermann, Versandhaus Neckermann, Frankfurt am Main, 1958–61, with circumferential walkways and sloping sunshades in textile covering. (Photo: Horstheinz Neuendorff. saai.)

Huppert, who had been involved in the planning in the office since the previous year and whom Eiermann now made site manager in Baden-Baden.[38] He was not only responsible for the organisation of the building site, but also for the planning of the interior finishing – the finish to which Eiermann attached the greatest importance, since for him the quality of each individual detail, as already quoted at the beginning, constituted what was actually noble in architecture. Eiermann thus stood in contrast to the rational functionalism that he liked to propagate in words, while in his work he was still entirely in the tradition of the ideas of the *Gesamtkunstwerk* of the dawning 20th century, which had been imparted to him by his teacher Hans Poelzig. Many dozens of sketches for detailed solutions preserved in Eiermann's estate as well as notes with requests and wishes from the architect to his colleague Huppert document the close communication in all questions arising in the further course of construction. And Huppert had the special ability to implement his boss's intentions to his complete satisfaction.

Building services

Construction photos reveal the great extent of the earthworks required on the slope after the demolition of the Krippenhof remains. In the chaos of the building site, however, the perfection of the shell of the building, characteristic of Eiermann, can already be seen. The terraces, the bulkhead-like cross-walls and closed outer walls were built in solid brick over concrete foundations. Thanks to the sophisticated planning, not a single visible brick had to be split, for Eiermann a principle of any design quality in building, which he also drilled into his students, from whom he demanded meticulous drawing of tiles and masonry plans as early as their basic studies. Empty pipes for the entire installation were already laid in the walls and concrete ceilings, which also required immense and precise preliminary planning work. In general, great importance was attached to the building services and their individual, not only technically but also formally satisfactory solution. The main lines of the electrical cables were laid in the cavity of the double-skin roof in an accessible way. Even the fuse panel in the cellar under the large living space has aesthetic qualities. The house bell is not operated by a button on the wall next to the entrance door, but by a device hanging from the cable from the canopy, like the emergency call button on a hospital bed, which Eiermann must have learned to appreciate during his long stay in hospital shortly before. Both parts of the house were fitted with underfloor heating powered by hot water; if required, infrared radiators could be switched on in the living rooms and bedrooms as a further source of heat. The radiators run through the living rooms and bedrooms in the suspended wooden ceilings as a linear design element. Their technical character with heating rod and chrome-plated reflectors is set in contrast to the natural wood and serves not only simply as a source of heat, but is also deliberately used to structure the room. The lighting is operated by means of pull switches, hemp ropes with specially turned round wooden handles in Oregon pine, which hang down from the ceiling. A bell system, designed as round plexiglass panes on the wall, can be used to make oneself known from every room in the kitchen, an astonishing afterlife of those bell pulls in noble villa households of the imperial era, which Eiermann must have remembered from his youth in Babelsberg. For hot summer days, Eiermann had also come up with a very unusual sprinkler system for cooling. A perforated water pipe running freely above the garden side of the roof in the large building dispensed water onto the corrugated parquet panels as needed.[39] The water not only cooled, however, it also offered a fascinating spectacle with a glittering curtain of falling drops as it flowed down over the widely protruding eaves.

Façades

In contrast to the solid masonry of the gable walls and the street façade of the main building, the garden façades are largely dissolved. This is achieved not only by means of room-high and room-wide glass surfaces in their natural wood frames, which are flush with the façade from the outside, but also by means of a scaffold-like spatial intermediate zone between inside and outside, which is presented to the fronts. Light, profiled concrete cantilever slabs at floor level and thin, white-painted metal rods, with hemp ropes attached to them at an angle to form a sunshade made of natural-coloured canvas, as well as the extremely overhanging roof made of corrugated terracotta panels with an ornamental corrugated edge, which is supported by narrow wooden rafters, visually lift the heaviness of the building.

Eiermann had first developed the perimeter façade with metal rods and integrated sun protection in 1953 during the construction of the Merkur department stores' in Reutlingen in order to facilitate the cleaning of the windows, which was only possible with great effort in the slightly earlier Merkur building in Heilbronn. After the special aesthetic quality of the scaffold-like construction had become apparent, Eiermann cultivated this solution, varying it from project to project. By the time of the German Pavilion at the World Exhibition in Brussels at the latest, the motif had become a trademark of his work. At the headquarters of the mail-order company Neckermann in Frankfurt, completed in 1961, fixed and slanted sun sails were integrated into the frame for the first time instead of movable blinds. Eiermann was to use this form again and again throughout his late work, right up to the Olivetti towers in Frankfurt, which were only completed posthumously. It was his most important contribution to contemporary architecture. In the 1960s and early 1970s, his type of perimeter façade was received internationally, although rarely with Eiermann's characteristic delicacy. In his own house, too, he attached great importance to the details of this diaphanous structure and strove to keep its design particularly filigree. The structural engineer, who criticised the insufficient load-bearing capacity of the construction and drew the attention of the building authorities to the fact that a payload of 100 kg/sqm had to be calculated for the balconies, meaning that they would have to be much more massive, was met with Eiermann's fierce wrath. In one of his infamous letters, he settled accounts with him, accusing him of bureaucratic stubbornness and accusing him of pursuing an unrealistic paragraph-riding.[40] He subsequently took matters into his own hands and obtained an exemption by denying the function as a balcony and declaring the projections in front of the windows to be flower shelves. In fact, stepping out onto the narrow walkway in front of the windows was intended, and not only for cleaning the glass. But they were in fact

che«.[42] Angesichts der Unstimmigkeiten, die es immer wieder mit dem Anrainer neben dem Atelierhaus gab, machte Eiermann das »Einigeln« zum Ziel: »Ich will keine Aussicht, keine Sonne, sondern Wände aus Grün«, vor allem in Richtung auf den Nachbarn, dem er mitteilte, er möge zur Kenntnis nehmen, daß ein »unbegehbarer Gürtel zwischen unsere beiden Grundstücke gelegt« und »eine Sichtverbindung praktisch ausgeschlossen« werde.[43] Der alte Baumbestand im unteren Grundstücksteil sollte auf jeden Fall erhalten bleiben, die weitere optische Abschirmung mit Hainbuchen, Haselnuß und Knöterich erfolgen, als Bodendecker unter den Bäumen wünschte er sich Heidelbeeren. Apfelbäume und eine Schattenmorelle sollten auf der stark abschüssigen Wiese wachsen – allesamt heimische Vegetation, nur nichts Exotisches, wie in Baden-Badener Villengärten eigentlich üblich. Als Pflanzen mit üppiger Blüte wollte er nur Kletter- und Hängerosen akzeptieren, die das Gestänge um die Terrassen vor dem Eßraum und der offenen Gartenloggia unter dem großen Wohnraum umspielen sollten.

Letztendlich wurde Jelinek nur als Berater für die Auswahl der Pflanzen herangezogen, eine gestalterische Aufgabe kam ihm kaum zu. Er war auch nicht für die Anpflanzung selbst zuständig, die an einen Baden-Badener Betrieb vergeben wurde. Mit dem wichtigsten tektonischen Gestaltungsmerkmal des Gartens, jener besonderen Treppe vom Haus hinunter zum Tauchbecken, hatte er sowieso nichts zu tun. Eiermann erklärte ihm seine Idee: »Die Wege sind keine Wege im übliche Sinne, sondern sind Betonkanalröhren, die mit Kies gefüllt werden, der mit Zement verfestigt wird, so daß man ähnlich wie in japanischen Gärten, von Stein zu Stein hüpft. Diese Röhren liegen also nicht mit dem Fußboden bündig, d. h. das könnte auch mal geschehen, sondern sie stehen stufenartig über dem fallenden Gelände heraus.« Zahlreiche Skizzen von Eiermann, die er seinem Bauleiter zur Realisierung seiner Vorstellungen schickte, haben sich zu diesem von ihm besonders geliebten Detail erhalten. Sie zeigen, wie wichtig es ihm war, daß einzelne Rohre auch bepflanzt und die Rohre selbst von einem Bett aus großen Kieseln begleitet werden sollten. In bachartigen, mit Kieseln bestückten Verläufen von unbefestigten Rinnen, die sich durch die Wiese am Hang ziehen, wird auch das Regen- und Beregnungswasser abgeleitet, das von den Dächern in Kiesschüttungen entlang der Gartenfront herunterfällt und nicht in der Kanalisation verschwindet, sondern auf dem unteren Grundstück versickert.

Farbigkeit

Das Haus Eiermann zeichnet sich durch eine ungewöhnliche Farbigkeit aus, mit Effekten, welche die historischen Schwarzweißphotos nicht wiedergeben können. In einem Brief an einen Malermeister in Kassel, mit dem das Büro beim Bau von Neckermann in Frankfurt gute Erfahrungen gemacht hatte und dem Eiermann deshalb auch die Malerarbeiten in Baden-Baden anvertraute, teilte er schon im Sommer 1961 mit, es könne sein, daß das gesamte Backsteinmauerwerk »innen wie außen mit einer einzigen Farbe behandelt wird, etwa dunkelblau«.[44] Die Entscheidung fiel schließlich für ein warmes dunkles Anthrazit, wobei der genaue Farbton und die Konsistenz der Farbe, die einen die Backsteine schlämmenden Charakter haben sollte, für den Architekten geradezu zur existenziellen Frage mutierte. Immer und immer wieder mußten Probeanstriche vor Ort angelegt werden, was angesichts des weiten Anfahrtsweges des Malers und des vollen Terminkalenders des Architekten ein kompliziertes Unterfangen wurde. Schließlich zeigte sich Eiermann zufrieden mit dem Ergebnis, das einerseits das amerikanische Oregon Pine der Fenster, Türen und Dachsparren in seinem rötlichen Farbton intensiver leuchtend in Erscheinung treten läßt, andererseits die beiden Baukörper in ihrer Körperlichkeit in die umgebende Landschaft einbettet. Daß weiße Neubauten die Landschaft »wie mit Haifischzähnen« zerstückeln würden, war ein gern von ihm formuliertes Bild.[45] Vom Kurpark auf der gegenüberliegenden Seite des Oostals

35. Egon Eiermann und Sep Ruf, Deutscher Pavillon auf der Weltausstellung 1958 in Brüssel, 1955–58, mit umlaufenden Umgängen und Jalousien als Sonnenschutz. (Photo: Eberhard Troeger. saai.)
36, 37. Egon Eiermann, Verwaltungs- und Ausbildungszentrum der Deutschen Olivetti, Frankfurt am Main, 1968 bis 1972, mit umlaufenden Umgängen und schräggestelltem Sonnenschutz in Textilbespannung. (Photo: Klaus Kinold. saai.)

35. Egon Eiermann and Sep Ruf, German Pavilion on the World's Fair 1958 in Brussels, 1955–58, with circumferential walkways and blinds as sun protection. (Photo: Eberhard Troeger. saai.)
36, 37. Egon Eiermann, administration and training centre of the Deutsche Olivetti, Frankfurt am Main, 1968–72, with circumferential walkways and sloping sunshades in textile covering. (Photo: Klaus Kinold. saai.)

also flower shelves, for the decorative row of circular recesses in the cantilever slabs was intended from the outset to accommodate commercially available clay pots planted with summer flowers. Most of the flowers were rampant nasturtiums with lush tendrils hanging down. In this way, Eiermann took up an old rural tradition of placing boards with sawn-out holes in front of parlour windows in farmhouses, into which flower pots could be placed in summer, allowing excess water to drip freely downwards through the hole in the bottom of the pot. And he also continued a motif of country house building from the beginning of his century, where flower borders in front of the windows played an important role as a design element, for example in the buildings of Josef Maria Olbrich on the Mathildenhöhe in Darmstadt.

Gardon

For Eiermann, house and garden formed a creative and ideal unit. This, too, was part of a bourgeois building culture that he had become acquainted with in the surroundings of his youth in Babelsberg before the First World War. For the planning of the gardens of his prewar Berlin houses, such as Haus Vollberg, he repeatedly called on the then still young garden architect Herta Hammerbacher, trained at Karl Foerster's Bornim School in nearby Potsdam. Her works show a near-natural, site-appropriate planting of shrubs, perennials and grasses, similar to the gardens of Eiermann's early houses, for which there is no evidence of a professional garden planner. There is a conspicuous absence of formal elements such as trimmed hedges or geometric and colourful flowerbeds, which were common in gardens in the 1920s. According to his own statements, he had the large surroundings of the Hardenberg Villa designed in a restrained manner in agreement with the building owner. It was important to him to present the building with its frame overgrown with knotweed detached on the lawn and to plant bushes as close as possible to the boundaries of the property in order to prevent people from looking in and to make unpopular neighbouring buildings disappear. Flowerbeds were not in demand there either.

When thinking about his own house, he turned to the garden architect Toni Jelinek in Frankfurt as early as spring 1961. Jelinek's garden design for the Feith House in the Lerchesberg residential area, for which Eiermann had contributed plans, had struck him as »clever and pretty«.[41] With Jelinek he hoped to gain an understanding of space, which, as he wrote to him, he felt many garden architects lacked. When the construction work had progressed accordingly in June 1962, he sent Jelinek a plot plan in which he had roughly drawn in the ideas he had developed together with Brigitte Eiermann. He rebuffed Jelinek's earlier ideas »as comical proposals [...] with taxus and similar hideous cemetery things«. He wanted anything but a fancy garden, »not a layout such as you may be used to through your Frankfurt clientele, but a natural and rather wild than tamed thing«.[42] In view of the disagreements that had repeatedly arisen with the neighbour next to the studio building, Eiermann made »unification« his goal: »I don't want a view, I don't want sun, I want walls of green«, especially in the direction of the neighbour, whom he told to take note of the fact that an »impassable belt would be placed between our two properties« and »a line of sight would be practically excluded«.[43] The old tree population in the lower part of the property was to be preserved at all costs, the further visual screening was to be done with hornbeam, hazel and knotweed, and he wanted blueberries as ground cover under the trees. Apple trees and a shade cherry should grow on the steeply sloping lawn – all native vegetation, just nothing exotic, as is actually customary in Baden-Baden villa gardens. He only wanted to accept climbing and hanging roses as plants with lush flowers, which were to play around the trellis around the terraces in front of the dining room and the open garden loggia under the large living room.

In the end, Jelinek was only called in as an advisor for the selection of plants; he was hardly given a design

fällt vom Haus eigentlich nur die horizontale Linie der Traufe des hellen Faserzementdachs auf. Aus der Nähe gesehen, erzielen die dünnen weißen Gestänge, die Sonnensegel und das Dach einen deutlichen graphischen Kontrast vor dem dunklen Fond der gemauerten Baukörper.

Bei den Nachbarn am Krippenhof war das Entsetzen groß, als im Juli 1962 der naturrote Backstein der Fassade und der Terrassen unter dem fast schwarzen Anstrich verschwand. Zu ungewohnt war eine solche Farbgebung in den frühen 1960er Jahren, als Weiß, versetzt mit einem leichten Grau-, Blau- oder Gelbstich, dem allgemeinen Geschmack entsprach. Offensichtlich beschwerte man sich sofort beim Bauordnungsamt, das seinerseits tätig wurde und die sofortige Einstellung der Malerarbeiten verlangte, da die Farbgebung nicht mit der Behörde abgestimmt worden sei. Eiermann reagierte empört mit dem ihm eigenen Selbstbewußtsein: »Ein solches Schreiben ist mir in meiner ganzen beruflichen Tätigkeit noch nicht zugegangen. Daß es ausgerechnet meinen persönlichen Bau betreffend in einem Lande geschieht, dessen Architektennachwuchs ich an der Technischen Hochschule dieses Landes erziehe und beeinflusse, berührt mich besonders merkwürdig, so daß ich hinter diesem Schreiben Kräfte am Werk sehe, die mit dem Kern der Dinge, um die es sich handelt, nichts zu tun haben.«[46] Mit dem Hinweis, er habe bei einem Empfang im Haus des Grafen Hardenberg mit Oberbürgermeister Schlapper gesprochen, und dieser habe seine Meinung begrüßt, daß sein Anwesen nicht in einem »konformistischen Weiß« der »ewig hellen Häuser« gestrichen werde, verlangte er, daß die Aufforderung zur Einstellung der Malerarbeiten zurückgezogen werde.

Sein Verweis auf das Stadtoberhaupt zog; seitens der Behörde wurde nun nichts weiter gegen die dunkle Farbe unternommen. Um so hartnäckiger zeigte das Amt sich jedoch im Hinblick auf die Auflage in der Baugenehmigung, das Faserzementdach im Ton engobierter Ziegel oder im Schieferton zu streichen, damit sich das Haus besser in die Bebauung des Viertels einfüge. Eiermann ließ die zementgrauen Platten auf der Unterseite des weiten Dachüberstands zwar streichen, aber keineswegs wie amtlich gefordert, sondern im Weiß des Gestänges, was immer wieder Schreiben der Baubehörde nach sich zog, die auf Erfüllung der in der Baugenehmigung fixierten Auflage pochten. 1966, fast vier Jahre nach dem Bezug des Hauses, bemühte Eiermann nochmals Oberbürgermeister Schlapper wegen der Forderungen, die er »nachgerade als Provokation« empfand. »Es ist doch wohl anzunehmen, daß das Haus, welches ich mir in der von Ihnen verwalteten Stadt baue, nicht eines der üblichen 08/15 werden kann. (…) Hier sind Kräfte am Werk, die mir den sonst so angenehmen Aufenthalt in Ihrer Stadt in einer solchen Weise verleiden, daß ich Sie davon in Kenntnis setzen muß. Ich darf Sie herzlich bitten, sich dieser Sache anzunehmen.«[47] Seit diesem Zeitpunkt ließ man Eiermann in der Farbfrage in Ruhe.

Innenausbau

Im Inneren des eigenen Domizils entfaltete Eiermann sein immenses kreatives Potential, das er bei anderen Bauaufgaben wie dem Verwaltungsbau eher rational zu zügeln trachtete und das er bei Kollegen scharf kritisieren konnte. Wie allenfalls noch beim Inneren der Gedächtniskirche, erlaubte sich Eiermann am eigenen Haus, sowohl Architekt als auch Künstler gleichzeitig zu sein. Das Ergebnis war ein Gesamtkunstwerk sondergleichen.

Der Grundriß des zweigeschossigen Hauses, wie er sich allmählich herauskristallisiert hatte, kommt mit seiner Erschließung durch einen langen innenliegenden Gang, an dem sich die gleichförmigen Zimmer auf der einen und die Nebenräume auf der anderen reihen, nicht besonders einfallsreich daher. Der große Wohnraum scheint nur angefügt zu sein, abgeschnitten vom restlichen Bau durch das Treppenhaus. Dennoch ist das dreidimensionale Raumerlebnis vor Ort in höchstem Maße komplex, ja geradezu manieriert. Die Treppe als Verbindungsglied zwischen den in Splitlevel gegeneinander versetzten Stockwerken ermöglicht überraschende Durchblicke von dort in den großen Wohn- sowie den Eßraum.

Bei den Deckenhöhen griff Eiermann, der in seiner Lehre oft als harscher Kritiker des Werkes von Le Corbusier auftrat, auf dessen Maßsystem Modulor zurück.[48] Die Höhe der Räume im Haupt- und Atelierhaus entsprechen der Modulor-Vorgabe von 2,26 m, das heißt, ein Mensch von 1,83 m Größe kann mit der Fingerspitze der ausgestreckten Hand die Decke gerade noch berühren – ein dem Goldenen Schnitt entsprechendes Verhältnis, aber auch ein Maß, das die baurechtliche Vorgabe für Raumhöhen im deutschen Wohnungsbau eigentlich um 4 cm unterschreitet. Freilich haben nicht alle Räume diese geringe Höhe. Die Wohn- und Schlafräume zwischen den Schottenwänden im Obergeschoß erhalten mehr Luftraum und in der Raumhierarchie auch mehr Bedeutung, indem die vom Dach abgehängten Holzdecken partiell den Dachraum miteinbeziehen. Beim großen Wohnraum ist dies ebenso. Als bedeutendster Raum des Hauses kommt ihm ein repräsentativer, hallenartiger Charakter zu, vor allem dadurch, daß der Fußboden wegen der Splitlevel-Anordnung der Etagen hier tiefer liegt als in den Obergeschoßräumen. Trotz des durchgehenden Daches über das gesamte Haus hinweg ist die Raumhöhe deshalb hier am größten. Die Modulorhöhe von 2,26 m wird aber auch in diesem Raum zitiert. Drei dünne horizontale Betonplatten, weiß gestrichen, durchziehen in dieser Höhe den Luftraum und gliedern ihn. Sie verbinden den frei stehenden, wie eine abstrakte Skulptur gestalteten offenen Kamin mit den Wänden. Auf diesem Zwischenboden stehende Grünpflanzen mit herunterhängenden Blatt-Trieben verleihen der Halle fast den Eindruck eines Wintergartens.

Wie der Kontrast zwischen geschlossenen und offenen Wänden im Äußeren, ist im Inneren der Gegensatz von nicht sehr groß dimensionierten Räumen mit bescheidenen Deckenhöhen und der Blick ins Weite, den die wandgroßen Glasöffnungen in den steil abfallenden Garten gewähren, von besonderer Eindrücklichkeit. Außen und innen verschmelzen. Der Einfluß der »fließenden Räume« von Mies van der Rohe ist zu spüren, wenngleich Eiermann mit seiner dreidimensional-gerüsthaften Fassade als Zwischenzone dem großen Vorbild Mies durchaus etwas Eigenes hinzuzufügen vermochte.

Beim Eßraum im unteren Geschoß, ein halbes Geschoß tiefer als der große Wohnraum und geöffnet gegen die Treppe, wird das Spiel mit dem Innen und Außen auf andere Weise zelebriert. Der enge und niedrige Raum zwischen den seitlichen Schottenwänden findet schwellenlos seine Verlängerung nach draußen in einer vorgelagerten podiumsartigen, hoch aus dem Garten

task. He was also not responsible for the planting itself, which was contracted out to a company in Baden-Baden. In any case, he had nothing to do with the most important tectonic design feature of the garden, that special staircase from the house down to the plunge pool. Eiermann explained his idea to him: »The paths are not paths in the usual sense, but are concrete channel tubes filled with gravel that is consolidated with cement, so that you hop from stone to stone, similar to Japanese gardens. So these tubes don't lie flush with the floor, which means that could happen sometimes, but they stick out like steps above the falling terrain.« Numerous sketches by Eiermann, which he sent to his site manager to realise his ideas, have survived on this detail, which he particularly loved. They show how important it was to him that individual pipes should also be planted and that the pipes themselves should be accompanied by a bed of large pebbles. In stream-like courses of unpaved gutters studded with pebbles and running through the meadow on the slope, the rain and sprinkling water is also drained away, falling from the roofs into gravel piles along the garden front and not disappearing into the sewage system but seeping away onto the lower plot.

Colour scheme

The Eiermann House is characterised by an unusual colour scheme, with effects that the historical black-and-white photographs cannot reproduce. In a letter to a master painter in Kassel, with whom the office had had a good experience during the construction of Neckermann in Frankfurt and to whom Eiermann therefore also entrusted the painting work in Baden-Baden, he informed Eiermann as early as the summer of 1961 that it might be possible for the entire brickwork »to be treated inside and out with a single colour, say dark blue«.[44] The decision was finally made in favour of a warm dark anthracite, whereby the exact shade and the consistency of the colour, which was to have a character that washed the bricks, became an existential question for the architect. Trial coats had to be applied over and over again on site, which became a complicated undertaking in view of the painter's long journey and the architect's busy schedule. In the end, Eiermann was satisfied with the result, which on the one hand allows the American Oregon pine of the windows, doors and rafters to appear more intensely luminous in its reddish hue, and on the other hand embeds the two buildings in their physicality in the surrounding landscape. That white new buildings would cut up the landscape »as if with shark's teeth« was an image he liked to formulate.[45] From the spa park on the opposite side of the Oostal valley, the only thing that actually stands out about the house is the horizontal line of the eaves of the light fibre-cement roof. Seen from close up, the thin white poles, the awnings and the roof achieve a clear graphic contrast against the dark background of the brick building.

The neighbours at Krippenhof were horrified when the natural red brick of the façade and the terraces disappeared under the almost black paint in July 1962. Such a colour scheme was too unusual in the early 1960s, when white, mixed with a slight grey, blue or yellow tinge, was the general taste. Obviously, people immediately complained to the building regulations office, which in turn took action and demanded that the painting work be stopped immediately, since the colour scheme had not been agreed with the authorities. Eiermann reacted indignantly with his characteristic self-confidence: »I have never received such a letter in my entire professional career. The fact that it concerns my personal building in a country whose young architects I educate and influence at the Technical University of this country touches me particularly strangely, so that I see forces at work behind this letter that have nothing to do with the core of the things it concerns.«[46] Saying that he had spoken to Lord Mayor Schlapper at a reception in the house of Count Hardenberg, and that the latter had welcomed his opinion that his property not be painted in a »conformist white« of the »eternally bright houses«, he demanded that the request to stop the painting work be withdrawn.

His reference to the head of the city was successful; the authorities did not take any further action against the dark colour. However, the authorities were all the more persistent with regard to the requirement in the building permit that the fibre-cement roof be painted in the tone of engobed tiles or slate, so that the house would fit in better with the buildings in the neighbourhood. Eiermann did have the cement-grey corrugated fibre-cement panels painted on the underside of the wide roof overhang, but not at all as officially required, but in the white of the frame, which repeatedly resulted in letters from the building authorities insisting on compliance with the requirement fixed in the building permit. In 1966, almmost four years after moving into the building, Eiermann again approached Mayor Schlapper about the demands, which he felt were »downright provocative«. »It can be assumed that the house I am building for myself in the city you administer cannot be one of the usual 08/15. (...) There are forces at work here that make my otherwise so pleasant stay in your city so unpleasant that I must inform you of them. I would like to ask you to take care of this matter.«[47] Since then, Eiermann has not been bothered about the colour issue any more.
[

Interior design

In the interior of his own domicile, Eiermann unfolded his immense creative potential, which he tended to curb rationally in other building tasks, such as the administrative building, and which he could sharply criticise in colleagues. As with the interior of the Memorial Church, Eiermann allowed himself to be both architect and artist at the same time. The result was an unparaleled synthesis of the arts.

The plan of the two-storey building, as it had gradually crystallised, does not appear particularly imaginative, with its development through a long interior corridor, along which the uniform rooms on one side and the adjoining rooms on the other are lined up. The large living room seems to be merely attached, cut off from the rest of the building by the staircase. Nevertheless, the three-dimensional spatial experience on site is highly complex, even mannered. The staircase as a connecting link between the floors, which are offset against each other in split levels, allows surprising views from there into the large living room and the dining room.

Eiermann, who was often a harsh critic of Le Corbusier's work in his teaching, used Le Corbusier's Modulor system of measurement for the ceiling heights.[48] The height of the rooms in the main building and studio building corresponds to the Modulor specification of

aufragenden gemauerten Terrasse. Diese wird von einem Gestänge umhegt, das von innen wie die Verlängerung der inneren Raumkanten wirkt. Ein im Sommer am Gestänge aufgehängter weißer Leinenvorhang schafft vollends die Illusion einer räumlichen Zusammengehörigkeit des Eßraums und seiner Verlängerung unter freiem Himmel.[49]

Außen und innen verbanden sich ursprünglich auch durch die einheitliche Farbe. Die meisten Sichtbacksteinwände waren innen im gleichen Anthrazit wie außen geschlämmt, auch in den Bädern und Toiletten, in der Küche und im Eßraum, wo selbst die niedrigen Sichtbetondecken von 2,26 m Höhe dunkel überstrichen waren. Nur einzelne Wände, vor allem solche, vor denen offene Regale und Betten standen, waren weiß gehalten, ebenso die Türblätter der Eingangstüren. Das überall präsente Oregon Pine des Holzwerks der inneren Dachschale im Obergeschoß und des großen hohen Wohnraums, bei den Fenstern sowie bei den Einbaumöbeln bildete dazu einen leuchtenden Kontrast, der dem Inneren eine ausgesprochen warmtonige wohnliche Atmosphäre verlieh. Kühl wirkenden Edelstahl duldete Eiermann nicht in seinem Haus. Er wollte Messingbeschläge an den Fenstern, brünierten Edelstahl bei den Türgriffen, und sogar für den Spiegel in der Garderobe mußte Kurt Huppert bräunlich getöntes Glas auftreiben, da »die Eiseskälte der normalen Spiegel dadurch vermieden wird, andererseits der menschliche Körper nicht in seiner albinohaften Scheußlichkeit sich spiegelt (leben ja nicht in Ischia)«, schrieb Eiermann an seinen Mitarbeiter.[50]

Eine große Rolle für die Gesamtwirkung des Hausinneren spielen die ungewöhnlich lebhaften, farbenfrohen Fußböden. Im ganzen Haus verwendete Eiermann einen keramischen Bodenbelag aus runden Fliesen von unterschiedlicher Größe, die es nicht katalogmäßig gab: Unglasierte Fliesen in naturrotem Ton sowie zahlreich eingestreute, in breiter Palette farbig glasierte Exemplare sind jeweils in dichter Anordnung in Estrich eingebettet. Ist das unregelmäßige, wie zufällig wirkende Verlegeschema auch durchgängig, so werden die einzelnen Räume durch die individuellen Anteile an unglasierten und glasierten Fliesen sowie deren Farbigkeit doch jeweils eindeutig definiert. So dominieren beispielsweise in den beiden Bädern des Obergeschosses weiße glasierte Rundfliesen, in die im Bad des Herrn blaue, im Bad der Dame gelbe Fliesen eingebunden sind. Vor Übergängen von einem Raum zum anderen können sich Fliesen in bestimmten Farben verdichten, um sich dann im anschließenden Raum allmählich wieder zu reduzieren. Bauleiter Kurt Huppert erhielt mittels Skizzen Anweisungen, wie das Prinzip der jeweils gewünschten Verlegung auszusehen hatte. Eiermanns Ziel war ein bunter, teppichhafter Eindruck, der auch direkte Naturassoziationen wecken sollte. Erstaunlich für einen technisch orientierten Modernisten wie Eiermann war sein Wunsch, auch blütenartige Rosetten in den Belag zu integrieren und diesen damit als Blumenwiese zu interpretieren. Die Rosetten bestehen aus einer Rundfliese, die jeweils von einem Kranz gleich großer und gleichfarbiger Fliesen umgeben ist, ein geradezu schlicht-naives Motiv, das an Kinderzeichnungen erinnert.

Nachdem künstlerisch gestaltete Keramikböden mit rechteckigen glasierten Fliesen schon in der Villa Hardenberg realisiert worden waren, plante Eiermann einen Mosaikboden mit Rundfliesen in verschiedenen Durchmessern und Farben sowie runden Betonplatten erstmals für den grandiosen Kirchenraum der Berliner Gedächtniskirche. In seinen Vorlesungen begründete er diese Lösung als die einzig mögliche, um in einem Oktogon mit seinen stumpfwinkligen Ecken Fliesen ohne Beschnitt verlegen zu können. Das Ergebnis muß ihn in gestalterischer Hinsicht so überzeugt haben, daß er dieses System auch in die strengen rechtwinkligen Räume seines Hauses übernahm, bei denen Rechteckplatten ohne Teilung hätten verlegt werden können.

Die runden Fliesen sind aber keineswegs ein Einzelmotiv. Rundformen ziehen sich als gestalterisches Leitmotiv durch das ganze Haus und seinen Garten: Runde Tontöpfe sind in die runden Löcher im Boden der Fassadenbalkone eingelassen, große runde Betonplatten mit wenigen glasierten Rundfliesen bedecken den Boden in der Gartenloggia unter dem großen Wohnraum, und die Terrasse davor hat ausschließlich runde Betonplatten, die in Kies gebettet liegen. Die runden Trittstufen der Gartentreppe verbreiten das Rundmotiv im Garten. Im Inneren sind die Klingelvorrichtungen in den Zimmern runde Scheiben, rund sind die Aussparungen für Blattpflanzen auf den Zwischendecken des großen Wohnraums sowie die Mattglasaugen in den Türblättern der Wohn- und Schlafräume, die nachts im Flur verraten, hinter welcher Tür noch Licht brennt. Rund sind auch die in den Fliesenbelag integrierten Fußabtreter an den Haustüren, der Wäscheabwurfschacht im Flur und die drei asymmetrischen Kochplatten des nach Sonderentwurf angefertigten Elektroherds in der Küche. Sogar die an der Rückwand der Gartenloggia in eigens vorgesehenen Nischen dekorativ gestapelten Rundhölzer aus gleich lang gesägten jungen Kiefernstämmen waren weniger als Heizmaterial für den Kamin im großen Wohnraum gedacht, denn als Teil der konsequent gestalteten Inszenierung des Architekten.[51]

Möblierung

Das Haus und seine Einrichtung sollten eine Einheit bilden, darüber herrschte bei Egon und Brigitte Eiermann Konsens. Bereits früh fiel daher die Entscheidung, daß nur Einzelmöbel, in erster Linie die nach eigenem Entwurf bei der Esslinger Firma Wilde & Spieth in Serie hergestellten Stühle sowie ebenfalls selbst entworfene Korbsessel und -sofas aus der Neureuter Wohnung nach Baden-Baden mitgenommen werden sollten.[52] Eine Ausnahme bildeten einige Thonet-Schaukelstühle, die Eiermann sehr schätzte und ebenfalls mitumzogen. Alle weitere Ausstattung wurde nach individuellem Maß für den jeweiligen Standort im Haus handwerklich neu angefertigt.

Der Entwurfsprozeß für Schränke, Betten, Bettkästen, Tische, Regale und die Küche verlief ähnlich wie jener für die Architektur. Eiermann machte eine Fülle von Skizzen, die von Kurt Huppert und anderen Büromitarbeitern in handgezeichnete Werkpläne für die ausführenden Handwerker umgesetzt wurden.[53] Wenn nötig, wurden eigens Zeichnungen im Maßstab 1:1 angefertigt, etwa für einen Teewagen, für Bilderrahmen, ein Gestell für das Clavichord oder Sockel für Plastiken, etwa einen Buddhakopf, der im Atelierhaus einen Blickpunkt auf einer Wandkonsole bildete. Die Sonderanfertigungen wurden größtenteils von der Firma Wilde & Spieth ausgeführt, seit 1949 Produzentin der erfolgreichen Serienmöbel nach Eiermanns Entwurf, wo man mit den Wünschen des Architekten aus langer intensiver Zusammenarbeit vertraut war. Das Mobiliar wurde keineswegs als Luxus-

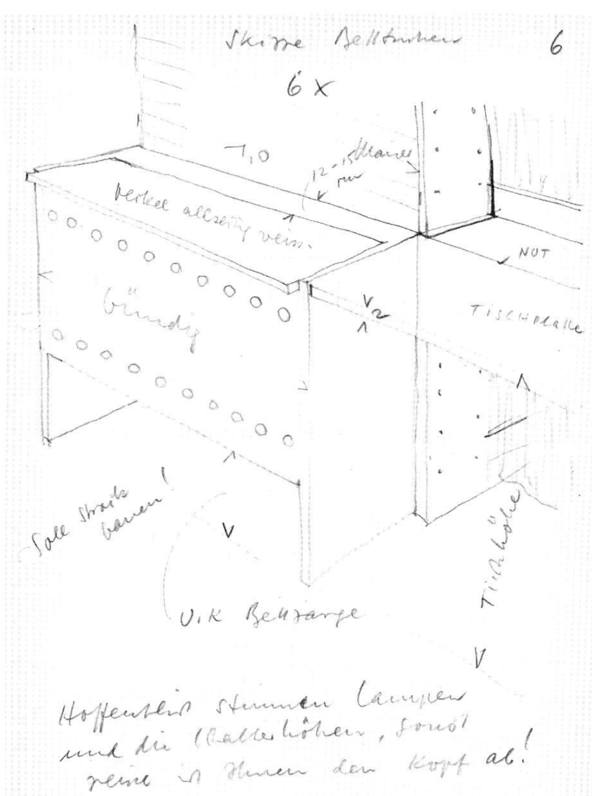

38. Egon Eiermann, Haus Eiermann, Baden-Baden, Skizze von Eiermann zur Gestaltung der Bett-Truhe im Wohn- und Schlafzimmer von Birgitte Eiermann. (saai.)

38. Egon Eiermann, Haus Eiermann, Baden-Baden, sketch by Eiermann for the bed-chest design in the living and bedroom of Birgitte Eiermann. (saai.)

2.26 m, which means that a person of 1.83 m height can just barely touch the ceiling with the fingertip of his outstretched hand – a ratio that corresponds to the golden section, but also a measurement that actually falls short of the building code specification for room heights in German housing by 4 cm. Admittedly, not all rooms have this low height. The living rooms and bedrooms between the bulkhead walls on the upper floor have more air space and also more significance in the room hierarchy, as the wooden ceilings suspended from the roof partially incorporate the roof space. This is also the case with the large living room. As the most important room in the building, it has a representative, hall-like character, above all because the floor is lower here than in the upper storey rooms due to the split-level arrangement of the storeys. Despite the continuous roof over the entire house, the room height is therefore greatest here. However, the modulor height of 2.26 m is also quoted in this room. Three thin horizontal concrete slabs, painted white, run through the air space at this height and divide it. They connect the free-standing open fireplace, designed like an abstract sculpture, with the walls. Green plants standing on this intermediate floor with leaf shoots hanging down give the hall almost the impression of a winter garden.

Like the contrast between closed and open walls on the outside, on the inside the contrast between not very large rooms with modest ceiling heights and the view into the distance afforded by the wall-sized glass openings into the steeply sloping garden is particularly impressive. Outside and inside merge. The influence of Mies van der Rohe's »flowing rooms« can be felt, even though Eiermann, with his three-dimensional, scaffold-like façade as an intermediate zone, was able to add something of his own to the great Mies model.

In the dining room on the lower floor, half a storey lower than the large living room and open to the staircase, the play with inside and outside is celebrated in a different way. The narrow, low space between the side bulkhead walls finds its extension to the outside without thresholds in a podium-like brick terrace rising high out of the garden. This is enclosed by a frame which, from the inside, looks like an extension of the inner edges of the room. A white linen curtain hung from the frame in summer completely creates the illusion of a spatial unity between the dining room and its open-air extension.[49]

The exterior and interior were originally also united by the uniform colour. Most of the exposed brick walls were painted the same anthracite colour on the inside as on the outside, also in the bathrooms and toilets, in the kitchen and in the dining room, where even the low exposed concrete ceilings of 2.26 m height were painted dark. Only individual walls, especially those in front of open shelves and beds, were kept white, as were the door leaves of the entrance doors. The Oregon pine of the woodwork of the inner roof shell on the upper floor and of the large, high living room, of the windows and of the built-in furniture, which was present everywhere, formed a luminous contrast that lent the interior a distinctly warm, homely atmosphere. Eiermann did not tolerate cool-looking stainless steel in his house. He wanted brass fittings on the windows, burnished stainless steel on the door handles, and even for the mirror in the cloakroom Kurt Huppert had to find brownish tinted glass, since »the icy coldness of normal mirrors is thereby avoided, and on the other hand the human body is not reflected in its albino-like hideousness (we don't live in Ischia)«, Eiermann wrote to his assistant.[50]

The unusually lively, colourful floors play a major role in the overall effect of the house interior. Throughout the house, Eiermann used a ceramic floor covering of round tiles of varying sizes that did not exist in a catalogue: unglazed tiles in natural red clay as well as numerous interspersed examples glazed in a wide range of colours are each embedded in screed in a dense arrangement. Even if the irregular, seemingly random laying pattern is consistent, the individual rooms are clearly defined by the individual proportions of unglazed and glazed tiles and their colours. For example, the two bathrooms on the upper floor are dominated by white glazed round tiles, with blue tiles in the gentleman's bathroom and yellow tiles in the lady's bathroom. Before transitions from one room to another, tiles in certain colours can become denser, only to gradually reduce again in the adjoining room. Site manager Kurt Huppert was given instructions by means of sketches as to how the principle of the desired laying was to look in each case. Eiermann's aim was to create a colourful, carpet-like impression that would also evoke direct associations with nature. Astonishing for a technically oriented modernist like Eiermann was his desire to also integrate flower-like rosettes into the covering and thus interpret it as a flower meadow. The rosettes consist of a round tile, each surrounded by a wreath of equally large and equally coloured tiles, a downright simple-naïve motif reminiscent of children's drawings.

After artistically designed ceramic floors with rectangular glazed tiles had already been realised in the Hardenberg Villa. Eiermann planned a mosaic floor with round tiles of different diameters and colours as well as round concrete slabs for the first time for the grandiose church hall of the Berlin Memorial Church. In his lectures, he justified this solution as the only one possible in order to be able to lay tiles without trimming in an octagon with its obtuse corners. The result must have convinced him so much from a design point of view that he also adopted this system in the strict right-angled rooms of his house, where rectangular tiles could have been laid without division.

The round tiles, however, are by no means a single motif. Round shapes run through the entire house and its garden as a design leitmotif: round clay pots are set into the round holes in the floor of the façade balconies, large round concrete slabs with a few glazed round tiles cover the floor in the garden loggia under the large living room, and the terrace in front of it has only round concrete slabs embedded in gravel. The round treads of the garden stairs extend the round motif in the garden. Inside, the bell fixtures in the rooms are round discs, round are the recesses for leafy plants on the false ceilings of the large living room, the frosted glass eyes in the door leaves of the living rooms and bedrooms, which at night in the hallway reveal which door still has a light on behind it. Also round are the doormats integrated into the tiling at the front doors, the laundry chute in the hallway, and the three asymmetrical hotplates of the custom-designed electric cooker in the kitchen. Even the round logs of young pine trunks sawn to the same length and stacked decoratively in specially provided niches on the back wall of the garden loggia were intended less as heating material for the fireplace in the large living room than as part of the architect's consistently designed staging.[51]

gut verstanden, sondern als funktionale Ergänzung zur Architektur, als Einbaumöbel eng mit dieser verbunden. Auch dafür wurde massives amerikanisches Oregon Pine verwendet, teilweise kombiniert mit weißen Kunststoffflächen aus Melaminharz, sich damit völlig in die Materialität und Farbigkeit der Architektur einfügend. Es sind einfache Konstruktionen, wie sie Eiermann ähnlich schon bei anderen Innenausbauten verwendet hatte, aber mit Anspruch an Solidität und Funktionalität. Akribisch machte sich Eiermann Gedanken über die Bedürfnisse des Alltags und dachte sich gerade im Hinblick auf Wäsche und Küchenutensilien außergewöhnliche Formen der Aufbewahrung aus. Die Wäsche- und Kleiderschränke im Obergeschoßflur sind in ihrer differenzierten Unterteilung besonders ausgefeilt, ebenso die Kücheneinrichtung im Haupthaus, aber auch die der kleinen separaten Studioküche im zweiten Obergeschoß des Atelierhauses. Diese wurden mit ziemlichem finanziellem Aufwand von der renommierten Karlsruher Möbelfirma Markstahler & Barth angefertigt.

Außergewöhnlich war auch die Art, in der die Wohn- und Schlafzimmer von Eiermann und seiner Frau im oberen Geschoß eingerichtet wurden. Die beiden Einzelbetten mit Truhen für das Bettzeug waren in den separaten Zimmern gleich gestaltet und gleich gestellt. Das architektonische Konzept der durch Schotten getrennten Einzelraumeinheiten war hier aber durchbrochen, da eine breite Öffnung in der gemauerten Zwischenwand die Zimmer miteinander verband. Man konnte jedoch nicht direkt vom einem in den anderen Raum gehen, weil auf jeder Seite ein schmales offenes Regal in die Leibung der Öffnung eingesetzt war, davor jeweils eine breite schreibtischartige Arbeitsplatte. In einem schmalen Zwischenraum zwischen den Regalen hing ein Vorhang, der zur Seite auf- und zugezogen werden konnte – ein theaterhaftes Spiel mit Offenheit und Geschlossenheit, mit Verbergen und Zeigen, das funktional nicht zu erklären ist.

Eiermanns Detailliebe und sein Perfektionismus verzögerten die Fertigstellung des Hauses immer wieder. So mußten beispielsweise an Tausenden von sichtbaren Messingschrauben der Bretter an den abgehängten Decken die Schlitze in dieselbe Richtung quer zur Hausachse gedreht werden. Zunehmend entnervt darüber, immer noch nicht fertig zu sein, schrieb er an seinen Bauleiter, er merke jetzt überhaupt erst, was er in seinem Leben als Architekt anderen Leuten zugemutet habe.[54] Im August 1962 war wenigstens das Ateliergebäude nutzbar. Der große Wunsch von Eiermann, seiner Frau gewissermaßen als Weihnachtsgeschenk das fertige Haus präsentieren zu können, ging zum Ende des gleichen Jahres dann tatsächlich in Erfüllung.

Reminiszenzen

Schon bald nach der Fertigstellung ist auf den latent japanischen Charakter von Architektur und Garten des Hauses Eiermann hingewiesen worden. Karin Kirsch hat diesen Aspekt in ihrem Buch *Die neue Wohnung und das alte Japan* von 1996 ausführlich analysiert. Auch Clemens Kieser ging im Zusammenhang mit seiner Beschäftigung mit der Einstufung des Anwesens als Kulturdenkmal von besonderer Bedeutung 2000 darauf ein, während Ulrich Coenen in seiner Artikelfolge über Eiermann 2022 in der *Baden-Badener Tageszeitung* dies als weniger relevant sah.[55] Tatsächlich sind Anklänge an das traditionelle japanische Haus nicht zu leugnen. Die flach geneigten, weit überstehenden und pagodenartig abgestuften Dächer ohne Dachrinnen, von denen bei Regen das Wasser in einigem Abstand vor den Fenstern wie ein Vorhang herunterfällt, das Ensemble von Haupt- und Nebenhaus überhaupt, wobei man letzteres als separates Teehaus interpretieren könnte, haben eine latente Affinität mit japanischer Baukunst, wenngleich Eiermann keineswegs direkt zitiert. Die Verwendung von raumhohen Schiebefenstern sowie Rahmenelementen mit quadratischem Gitterwerk, die vor die geöffneten Fenster geschoben werden können, die additive, leichte Struktur und die Verwendung von Holz, aber auch generell die Beziehung von gestaltetem Innen- zu gestaltetem Außenraum – all diese Charakteristika können als Umsetzung alt-japanischer Bauprinzipien interpretiert werden. Als unmittelbarste Rezeption ist freilich die Treppe mit den runden Trittsteinen vom Haus hinunter zum Tauchbecken im Garten anzusehen. In der erhalten ge-

39. Katsura-Villa, Kyoto, vollendet 1645. (Photo: KimonBerlin.)
40. Trittsteine im Garten des ersten Kaiserpalastes in Kyoto. (Photo: Daderot.)
41. Egon Eiermann, Haus Eiermann, Baden-Baden, die Trittsteine im Garten. (Photo: Horstheinz Neuendorff. saai.)
42. Egon Eiermann, Haus Eiermann, Baden-Baden, der Garten mit den das Gelände durchquerenden Trittsteinen. (Photo: Horstheinz Neuendorff. saai.)

39. Katsura Villa, Kyoto, completed 1645. (Photo: KimonBerlin.)
40. Stepping stones in the garden of the first imperial palace in Kyoto. (Photo: Daderot.)
41. Egon Eiermann, Eiermann House, Baden-Baden, the stepping stones in the garden. (Photo: Horstheinz Neuendorff.saai.)
42. Egon Eiermann, Eiermann House, Baden-Baden, the garden with the stepping stones crossing the grounds. (Photo: Horstheinz Neuendorff. saai.)

Furnishing

Egon and Brigitte Eiermann agreed that the house and its furnishings should form a unity. It was therefore decided early on that only individual pieces of furniture, primarily the chairs mass-produced to their own design by the Esslingen firm Wilde & Spieth, as well as wicker armchairs and sofas also designed by Eiermann himself, were to be taken from the Neureut flat to Baden-Baden.[52] An exception were a few Thonet rocking chairs, which Eiermann greatly appreciated and also moved with him. All other furnishings were handcrafted according to individual measurements for the respective location in the house.

The design process for wardrobes, beds, bed frames, tables, shelves and the kitchen was similar to that for the architecture. Eiermann made an abundance of sketches, which were converted by Kurt Huppert and other office staff into hand-drawn working plans for the craftsmen carrying out the work.[53] If necessary, drawings were made on a scale of 1:1, for example for a tea trolley, for picture frames, a stand for the clavichord or pedestals for sculptures, such as a Buddha's head, which formed a focal point on a wall console in the studio building. Most of the custom-made furniture was produced by the firm Wilde & Spieth, which had been producing the successful series of furniture based on Eiermann's design since 1949, and which was familiar with the architect's wishes from many years of intensive collaboration. The furniture was by no means seen as a luxury item, but as a functional complement to the architecture, closely linked to it as built-in furniture. Solid American Oregon pine was also used for this, partly combined with white plastic surfaces made of melamine resin, thus blending in completely with the materiality and colourfulness of the architecture. These are simple constructions, similar to those Eiermann had already used for other interior fittings, but with a demand for solidity and functionality. Eiermann thought meticulously about the needs of everyday life and came up with unusual forms of storage, especially with regard to laundry and kitchen utensils. The linen and clothes cupboards in the upper floor corridor are particularly sophisticated in their differentiated subdivisions, as is the kitchen equipment in the main building, but also that of the small separate studio kitchen on the second floor of the studio building. These were made at quite a financial cost by the renowned Karlsruhe furniture company Markstahler & Barth.

The way in which the living rooms and bedrooms of Eiermann and his wife on the upper floor were furnished was also unusual. The two single beds with chests for the bedding were designed and placed in the same way in the separate rooms. The architectural concept of individual room units separated by bulkheads was broken here, however, as a wide opening in the brick partition wall connected the rooms. However, it was not possible to go directly from one room to the other, because on each side a narrow open shelf was inserted into the reveal of the opening, in front of which was a wide desk-like worktop. In a narrow space between the shelves hung a curtain that could be opened and closed to the side – a theatrical way of playing with openness and closure, with concealing and showing, that cannot be explained functionally.

Eiermann's attention to detail and his perfectionism repeatedly delayed the completion of the house. For example, the slots on thousands of visible brass screws of the boards on the suspended ceilings had to be turned in the same direction across the axis of the house. Increasingly exasperated at still not being finished, he wrote to his site manager that he was only now realising what he had put other people through in his life as an architect.[54] In August 1962, at least the studio building was usable. Eiermann's great wish to be able to present the finished house to his wife as a Christmas present, so to speak, was actually fulfilled at the end of the same year.

Reminiscences

Soon after its completion, the latent Japanese character of the architecture and garden of the Eiermann House was pointed out. Karin Kirsch analysed this aspect in detail in her 1996 book *Die neue Wohnung und das alte Japan*. Clemens Kieser also addressed this in connection with his preoccupation with the classification of the

bliebenen Notiz an seinen Bauleiter bezieht der Architekt sich bei dieser Idee namentlich auf japanische Gärten, wo man »von Stein zu Stein hüpft«.[56] Und noch aus einer anderer Quelle wird sein Interesse an japanischen Gewohnheiten deutlich, die ihn während der Entwurfs- und Bauphase seines Hauses umtrieben. In einem Brief an den Malermeister, der den Sichtbeton der Stufen der Innentreppe nur dünn lasieren sollte, schrieb Eiermann, daß »in diesem Haus, ähnlich wie in Japan, nur Strohschuhe getragen würden«.[57] Es sei deshalb kein Abrieb der Farbe durch Straßenschuhe zu befürchten.

Eiermanns Affinität zu Japan und dessen traditioneller Baukultur reicht bis in die 1930er Jahre zurück, und diese persönliche Zuneigung wurde über Literatur geweckt, die damals erschien und in Kreisen innovativ denkender Architekten auf fruchtbaren Boden fiel, die sich in ihren Positionen durch die fernöstliche Tradition bestätigt fühlten. Eiermann dürfte Bruno Tauts 1936 erschienene Publikation *Grundlinien Japanischer Architektur* gekannt haben, Tetsuro Yoshidas Buch *Das Japanische Wohnhaus* besaß er nachweislich in seiner ersten Auflage aus dem Jahr 1935, und es scheint für ihn eine Offenbarung gewesen zu sein.[58] Es gehörte nämlich 1947 zu seinen ersten Tätigkeiten als frisch berufener Professor an der TH Karlsruhe, die Bibliothek der Architekturfakultät aufzufordern, diese bedeutende Publikation zu erwerben, da ihm sein Exemplar in den Wirren des Krieges verlorengegangen sei.[59] Das 1939–42 erbaute Haus Vollberg in Berlin ist in seiner flach-gruppierten Bauweise, seiner Materialität, seinem Bezug der Innenräume auf die Gartenhöfe sowie der ungewöhnlichen Verwendung von separat liegenden Trittsteinen vor den Türöffnungen ins Freie nur vor dem Hintergrund des Einflusses der Photographien von Yoshida zu verstehen, die auf Eiermann großen Eindruck gemacht haben.

Die schlichte, wohlproportionierte Ästhetik der alten Kunst Japans hat ihn als ästhetisches Phänomen ein Leben lang fasziniert, wenn es auch keine wirklich tiefgreifende Auseinandersetzung mit der Kultur des Landes gegeben hat. Eine Reise nach Fernost war laut Brigitte Eiermann in den 1960er Jahren ein stets gehegter Traum, der sich jedoch nie verwirklichen ließ. Ein gewisser Ersatz bildete in den letzten Lebensjahren für Eiermann die Freude, eine Sammlung japanischer Netsuke zusammenzutragen, kleine figürliche oder verzierte Anhänger aus Metall, Holz, Elfenbein oder Horn, die am Gürtel traditioneller Kimonos als Gegengewicht für die Befestigung von kleinen Behältern oder anderen Gegenständen getragen wurden.[60]

Aber noch eine zweite, sehr persönliche Vorliebe sollte ihre Spuren in Eiermanns Haus hinterlassen – sein besonderes Faible für Schiffe und das Segeln. Schon als Schüler kreuzte er nahe seines Elternhauses in Babelsberg auf dem Griebnitzsee, der Havel und dem Wannsee. Mit ersten Einnahmen kaufte er sich ein eigenes Segelboot, das sein größter Stolz war und mit dem er auch an Regatten teilnahm. Als Mitglied einer Berliner Mannschaft gewann er in den 1930er Jahren sogar das »Blaue Band vom Balaton« im längsten europäischen Segeltörn auf einem Binnengewässer, einer seit 1934 stattfindenden internationalen Rundregatta auf dem ungarischen Plattensee.[61] Aber auch Ozeandampfer hatten es ihm wie vielen Zeitgenossen angetan. 1937 lernte er nach dem Besuch der Pariser Weltausstellung auf einer längeren Kreuzfahrt rund um Frankreich und Spanien die Baulichkeiten und das Leben auf solch einer schwimmenden Stadt in eigener Anschauung kennen und schätzen. Nach dem Weltkrieg zog er es vor, per Schiff auf einer der großen Transatlantiklinien in die USA zu reisen statt mit dem Flugzeug zu fliegen, wenn es sich zeitlich nur irgendwie machen ließ.[62] Das Schiffserlebnis sollte sich in seiner Architektur niederschlagen. Die mit einer Reling umgebene Dachterrasse auf der 1938/39 errichteten Feuerlöscherfabrik in Apolda, auf der die Angestellten auf Liegestühlen unter einem Flugdach wie auf einem Schiffsdeck ihre Mittagspause verbringen konnten, ist als direkte Reminiszenz seines Erlebens der Schiffsreise vom Vorjahr zu verstehen.

Eiermann bedauerte es, daß seine Berufung nach Karlsruhe ihm keine Möglichkeiten mehr bot, in der Nähe seiner Segelleidenschaft nachzugehen. Sein Boot, das den Weltkrieg in Berlin wie durch ein Wunder unbeschadet überstanden hatte, schenkte er seinem Sohn, der dort zeitweise bei seiner Mutter lebte.[63] Die Bootsmetaphorik sollte aber bei der Gestaltung seines Hauses eine nicht unwichtige Rolle spielen. Schon der mit einem extravagant weit auskragenden Vordach versehene Eingang in das obere Haus ist wie ein Landungssteg inszeniert. Das Haus wirkt für den Besucher, der von der Straße kommt, wie »angedockt«. Auf dem Podest zwischen der schmalen und recht steilen Betontreppe und der Haustür steht man auf einem lamellenartigen Holzrost, der seinerseits über einer Kiesschüttung in einer Aussparung der Betonkonstruktion ruht. Ein gewisses Gefühl von Unsicherheit stellt sich ein, wenn man über diese Zäsur geht, wie der Schritt über einen hölzernen Steg auf ein Boot. Beim Hinaufgehen der sieben Treppenstufen wird man zudem zur Rechten und zur Linken von weiß lackiertem, relingartigem Gestänge begleitet, das am Haus selbst nur wie eingesteckt erscheint, wie jederzeit wieder zu lösen. Zwei dreieckige Segel aus naturfarbenem Segeltuch sind daran aufgespannt, festgezurrt mit einem durch Ösen geschlungenen Seil, die Ecken verstärkt mit Leder, fixiert mit Lederlaschen. Am linken Segel ist außerdem eine Tasche aus Segeltuch befestigt, die als Briefkasten des Hauses fungiert. All dies sind Elemente, die aus der Welt des Segelns bekannt sind. Auch im Blick aus den Wohnräumen hinaus in den Garten ist Segeltuch und Seiltakelage, ursprünglich aus den Naturprodukten Segelleinen beziehungsweise Hanf, als Reminiszenz an die Seglerwelt immer präsent, sind doch die schräg gestellten Lamellen des Gestänges zum Sonnenschutz damit bespannt. Zur Bestätigung der Schiffskonnotation hat Eiermann für ein altes Schiffsmodell, das er offensichtlich besonders in Ehren hielt, in seinem Haus einen symbolträchtigen Ort zugedacht. Eine Entwurfsskizze belegt, daß er es schon in der Planungsphase als festen Wandschmuck für den Eingangsbereich vorgesehen hatte. Endgültig fand es seinen Platz im Wandfeld über der Haustür als hervorgehobene Supraporte, und dort befindet es sich erfreulicherweise noch heute. Der Blick eines jeden, der das Haus verläßt, muß unwillkürlich auf dieses Objekt fallen.

Die Rezeption

Im Frühsommer 1963, ein halbes Jahr nach Bezug des Hauses, ließ Egon Eiermann sein jüngstes Werk professionell photographieren. Horstheinz Neuendorff, als Berufsphotograph in Baden-Baden ansässig, machte in seinem Auftrag Dutzende von künstlerisch anspruchsvollen Aufnahmen des Äußeren und Inneren – bei der Motivauswahl, den Bildausschnitten und der Retusche

property as a cultural monument of special significance in 2000, while Ulrich Coenen saw this as less relevant in his series of articles on Eiermann in the Baden-Baden daily newspaper in 2022.[55] Indeed, echoes of the traditional Japanese house are undeniable. The shallowly pitched, widely overhanging and pagoda-like stepped roofs without gutters, from which the water falls down like a curtain at some distance in front of the windows when it rains, the ensemble of main and side building in general, whereby the latter could be interpreted as a separate teahouse, have a latent affinity with Japanese architecture, although Eiermann by no means quotes directly. The use of floor-to-ceiling sliding windows and frame elements with square latticework that can be slid in front of the open windows, the additive, light structure and the use of wood, but also generally the relationship between designed interior and designed exterior space – all these characteristics can be interpreted as the implementation of ancient Japanese building principles. The staircase with the round stepping stones from the house down to the plunge pool in the garden can be regarded as the most immediate reception. In the surviving note to his construction supervisor, the architect refers to Japanese gardens, where one »jumps from stone to stone«.[56] And yet another source reveals his interest in Japanese customs, which were his preoccupation during the design and construction phases of his house. In a letter to the master painter who was to apply only a thin glaze to the exposed concrete of the steps of the interior staircase, Eiermann wrote that »in this house, similar to Japan, only straw shoes would be worn«.[57] There was therefore no need to fear abrasion of the paint by street shoes.

Eiermann's affinity for Japan and its traditional building culture goes back to the 1930s, and this personal affection was awakened via literature that appeared at the time and fell on fertile ground in circles of innovative-minded architects who felt their positions confirmed by the Far Eastern tradition. Eiermann must have been familiar with Bruno Taut's publication *Grundlinien Japanischer Architektur*, published in 1936, and he demonstrably owned the first edition of Tetsuro Yoshida's book *Das Japanische Wohnhaus*, published in 1935, and it seems to have been a revelation for him.[58] In 1947, one of his first activities as a newly appointed professor at the TH Karlsruhe was to ask the library of the architecture faculty to acquire this important publication, as his copy had been lost in the turmoil of war.[59] The Vollberg House in Berlin, built in 1939–42, in its flat-grouped construction, its materiality, its reference of the interiors to the garden courtyards, and the unusual use of free lying stepping stones in front of the doorways to the outdoors, can only be understood against the background of the influence of Yoshida's photographs, which seem to have made a great impression on Eiermann.

The simple, well-proportioned aesthetics of Japan's ancient art fascinated him as an aesthetic phenomenon throughout his life, even if there was no really profound engagement with the country's culture. According to Brigitte Eiermann, a trip to the Far East was a constantly cherished dream in the 1960s, but one that could never be realised. A certain substitute in the last years of Eiermann's life was the pleasure of assembling a collection of Japanese netsuke, small figural or decorated pendants made of metal, wood, ivory or horn that were worn on the belt of traditional kimonos as a counterweight for holding small containers or other objects.[60]

But a second, very personal preference was to leave its mark on Eiermann's home – his particular penchant for ships and sailing. Even as a schoolboy, he cruised near his parental home in Babelsberg on the Griebnitzsee, the Havel and the Wannsee. With his first earnings, he bought his own sailing boat, which was his greatest pride and with which he also took part in regattas. As a member of a Berlin crew, he even won the »Blue Ribbon of Lake Balaton« in the 1930s in the longest European sailing trip on an inland waterway, an international round-robin regatta on Lake Balaton in Hungary, which had been taking place since 1934.[61] But ocean liners also appealed to him, as they did to many contemporaries. In 1937, after visiting the Paris World's Fair, he went on a long cruise around France and Spain and got to know and appreciate the buildings and life on such a floating city first-hand. After the World War, he preferred to travel to the USA by ship on one of the major transatlantic routes rather than flying by plane, if only time permitted.[62] The ship experience was to be reflected in his architecture. The roof terrace surrounded by a railing on the fire-extinguisher factory in Apolda, built in 1938/39, where the employees could spend their lunch break on deck chairs under a flying roof as if on a ship's deck, is to be understood as a direct reminiscence of his experience of the previous year's ship voyage.

Eiermann regretted that his appointment to Karlsruhe no longer offered him the opportunity to pursue his passion for sailing in the vicinity. He gave his boat, which had miraculously survived the World War in Berlin unscathed, to his son, who lived there temporarily with his mother.[63] However, the boat metaphor was to play a not unimportant role in the design of his house. Even the entrance to the upper house, with its extravagantly wide overhanging canopy, is staged like a landing stage. For the visitor coming from the street, the house appears to be »docked«. On the landing between the narrow and quite steep concrete staircase and the front door, one stands on a slat-like wooden grating, which in turn rests over a gravel fill in a recess in the concrete structure. A certain feeling of insecurity sets in when one steps over this caesura, like stepping over a wooden footbridge onto a boat. As one climbs the seven steps, one is also accompanied on the right and left by white-painted, railing-like rods, which only appear to be plugged into the house itself, as if they could be unplugged at any time. Two triangular sails made of natural-coloured canvas are stretched on it, lashed with a rope looped through eyelets, the corners reinforced with leather, fixed with leather straps. A canvas bag is also attached to the left sail, which functions as the house's letterbox. All these are elements familiar from the world of sailing. Even when looking out of the living rooms into the garden, sailcloth and rope rigging, originally made of the natural products sailcloth and hemp respectively, are always present as a reminiscence of the sailing world, since the slanted slats of the frame for sun protection are covered with them. To confirm the ship connotation, Eiermann has provided a symbolic place in his house for an old model of a ship that he obviously held in particularly high esteem. A sketch of the design shows that even during the planning phase he had intended it to be a permanent wall ornament in the entrance area. It finally found its place in the wall panel above the front door as a highlighted supraport, and fortunately it is still there today. The gaze of anyone leaving the house must involuntarily fall on this object.

von Nachbarbauten sicherlich in enger Abstimmung mit dem Architekten, dem die Bilddokumentation seiner Neubauten immer ein großes Anliegen war, das er sich viel Geld kosten ließ. Neuendorff hatte spätestens seit dem Vorjahr mit seinen Aufnahmen der Villa Hardenberg und der Neckermann-Zentrale jene Rolle des bevorzugten Photographen für Eiermann übernommen, die bis dahin seit Berliner Zeiten Eberhard Troeger innehatte.[64] Aus gesundheitlichen Gründen wollte jener jedoch nach 1958, als er für Eiermann noch einmal in großem Umfang tätig gewesen war und den Deutschen Pavillon auf der Brüsseler Weltausstellung für die Nachwelt festgehalten hatte, keine größeren Aufträge mehr fern seines Wohnorts Hamburg annehmen. Wie zu Troeger sollte sich nach 1960 auch zu dem ebenfalls aus Berlin stammenden Neuendorff und dessen Frau auf privater Ebene ein freundschaftliches Verhältnis entwickeln, das bis zum Tod des Architekten bestand. Eiermann schätzte die Arbeiten von Neuendorff, dessen Schwarzweißphotographie in kräftigen Kontrasten seinen Vorstellungen entgegenkam. Umgekehrt verstand der Photograph schnell, was der Architekt wollte. Und er sollte bis zu den erst nach seinem Tod fertiggestellten Gebäuden für IBM in Stuttgart und Olivetti in Frankfurt alle seine neuen Werke dokumentieren.

Die Neuendorff-Photos dienten Eiermann in erster Linie als Gewähr dafür, daß sein Haus in der von ihm gewünschten Weise in Fachzeitschriften veröffentlicht wurde. Die Aufnahmen, vom Büro eigens gezeichnete Publikationspläne sowie einen Text von Brigitte Eiermann, aus dem eingangs zitiert wurde, stellte er allen interessierten Redaktionen zur Verfügung. Nichts wollte er dem Zufall überlassen. Bereits Mitte 1963 erschien in seinem Sinn ein umfangreich bebilderter Artikel in *Architektur und Wohnform*, und nachdem das in Mailand erscheinende *Architectural Annual Lotus* 1964 das Haus Eiermann in seiner Zusammenstellung der vierzig bedeutendsten Beispiele für aktuelle Wohnhäuser weltweit eingereiht hatte, sollte das Haus in zahlreichen deutschen, englischen, französischen sowie italienischen Zeitschriften abgebildet und besprochen werden.[65] Es dürfte nicht zuletzt deshalb breite Aufmerksamkeit gefunden haben, weil es in einem gewissen Gegensatz stand zu den in den 1960er Jahren vorherrschenden neoexpressiven und brutalistischen Strömungen in der Baukunst. Aber auch nachdem das Haus mit den Jahren seine Neuheit eingebüßt hatte, wurde seine Bedeutung als Klassiker der zeitgenössischen Architektur anerkannt. Wolfgang Pehnt nahm es 1970 in sein Kompendium *Neue Deutsche Architektur 3* auf, und immer wieder wurde und wird es in Einrichtungszeitschriften präsentiert, ist Sujet in wissenschaftlichen Publikationen, 2002 zusammen mit der Villa Hardenberg sogar Thema einer eigenen Ausstellung des Bundes Deutscher Architekten in Baden-Baden, und 2022 widmete Ulrich Coenen eine 14teilige Artikelfolge in der Baden-Badener Lokalpresse dem Haus Eiermann, der Villa Hardenberg und der Verbindung des Architekten mit der Stadt. Wie Studenten der 1960er Jahre überliefern, scheint Eiermann Aspekte seines Domizils wiederholt in Vorlesungen behandelt zu haben. Für sie, die in ihrem Studium als zentrale Arbeit zur Aufgabe hatten, »das eigene Haus« zu entwerfen, war die Neugierde groß, zu erfahren, wie ihr charismatischer Lehrer wohnte. Man pilgerte geradezu nach Baden-Baden, und man schätzte sich glücklich, wenn sich die Gelegenheit bot, auch einen Blick ins Innere zu werfen.

Die Entwicklung bis heute

Sehr viel scheint Eiermann von seinem Domizil in den siebeneinhalb Jahren, die ihm bis zu seinem Tod blieben, nicht gehabt zu haben. Als viel beschäftigter Architekt von Großprojekten wie der Deutschen Botschaft in Washington oder dem Abgeordnetenhochhaus in Bonn, als Star der deutschen Architekturszene, als gefragter Preisrichter, als Mitglied in Kommissionen und als Hochschullehrer war er trotz angeschlagener Gesundheit ständig unterwegs.[66] Wenn er erschöpft nach Hause kam, zog er sich gerne in das Atelierhaus zurück, wo er meist auch schlief. Den großen Wohnraum nutzte er fast nur zum Hören von Barockmusik und Jazz auf der damals modernsten Braun-Stereoanlage. Wie Tochter Anna Eiermann berichtet, war dieser Raum ähnlich dem Salon einer Villa des 19. Jahrhunderts für sie und ihre Schulfreundinnen tabu. Große gesellschaftliche Ereignisse fanden in diesem repräsentativen Ambiente allerdings ebenfalls kaum statt. Das Clavichord, das 1954 in der von Eiermann gestalteten deutschen Abteilung auf der Triennale in Mailand gezeigt worden war und danach in seinen Besitz überging, wurde selten gespielt. Wenn Familienleben stattfand, dann am ehesten am Tisch im Eßraum mit der Durchreiche zur Küche. Dort durften aber keine Papierservietten liegen, sonst fing Eiermann sofort an, darauf Einfälle zu skizzieren und war kaum mehr ansprechbar.

Die Organisation von Haus und Garten, Aufgabe von Brigitte Eiermann, erwies sich als aufwendig. Schon das tägliche Gießen der vielen einzelnen Blumentöpfe auf den Balkonen war im Sommer eine Herausforderung, wobei das durch die Löcher der Töpfe nach unten tropfende Wasser regelmäßig die Scheiben der Fenster im Geschoß darunter verschmutzte. Der Abfluß des Regenwassers im Garten machte ebenso als Problem. Vor ihrer Fixierung mit Beton wurden die groben Kiesel in den schmalen Wasserrinnen durch das Gras bei jedem starken Regenguß den Steilhang hinuntergespült und mußten mühsam wieder an ihren Ort zurückgeschafft werden. Wenig funktional war auch die Plazierung des Herdes in der Küche. Fett spritzte beim Braten auf die nur schwer zu reinigende Jalousie unmittelbar dahinter, mit der die Durchreiche geschlossen wurde. Öffnete man diese, um sie vor Verschmutzung zu bewahren, zogen die Küchengerüche ungehindert in den Eßraum. Eine Haushälterin wurde eingestellt, die in die separat erschlossene Einliegerwohnung im unteren Geschoß zog, wo ursprünglich Eiermanns Mutter hätte einziehen sollen. Eine Art Hausmeister kam einmal in der Woche, um gröbere Arbeiten in Haus und Garten zu erledigen. Relativ schnell zeigte sich auch ein gravierender Bauschaden. Die Backsteine erwiesen sich im Bereich der Terrassen sowie beim Wasserbecken im Garten – immer dort, wo dahinter Erdreich anstand – entgegen der Beteuerungen des Herstellers als nicht frostsicher. Die Farbe hielt nicht auf dem Untergrund, Teile der Oberflächen der Steine platzten ab. Die Schäden sind bereits auf Photos der Mitte der 1960er Jahre nicht zu übersehen.

Im Juli 1970 erlitt Eiermann im Alter von nur 65 Jahren einen weiteren Herzinfarkt. Wie beim ersten im Jahr 1960, als er wegen des Baus der Gedächtniskirche unter großem Druck stand, waren es jetzt die Großprojekte für IBM und Olivetti, die ihn über Gebühr beanspruchten. Er starb auf dem Rücksitz seines Autos auf der Autobahn, seine Frau fuhr ihn gerade von einer Routineuntersuchung im Krankenhaus, die eigentlich ein günstiges

43. Egon Eiermann im eigenen Segelboot, 1930er Jahre. (saai.)
44. Segel am Eingang des Hauses Eiermann, Baden-Baden, 1963. (Photo: Horstheinz Neuendorff. saai.)
45. Der Eingang des Hauses Eiermann, Baden-Baden, als Bootssteg, 2023. (Photo: Gerhard Kabierske.)

43. Egon Eiermann in his own sailing boat, 1930s. (saai.)
44. Sails at the entrance to the Eiermann House, Baden-Baden, 1963 (Photo: Horstheinz Neuendorff. saai.)
45. The entrance to the Eiermann House, Baden-Baden, as a landing stage, 2023. (Photo: Gerhard Kabierske.)

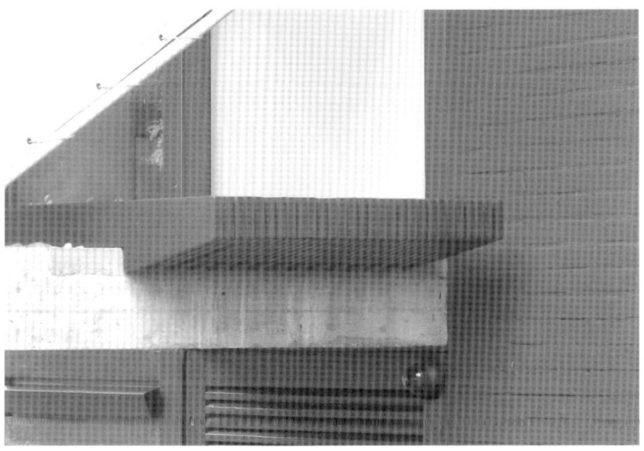

The reception

In the early summer of 1963, half a year after moving into the house, Egon Eiermann had his latest work professionally photographed. Horstheinz Neuendorff, a professional photographer based in Baden-Baden, was commissioned to take dozens of artistically sophisticated photographs of the exterior and interior – the choice of motifs, the cropping of the pictures and the retouching of neighbouring buildings certainly in close consultation with the architect. The pictorial documentation of his new buildings was always a major concern for him that cost him a lot of money. Since the previous year at the latest, Neuendorff had taken on the role of Eiermann's preferred photographer with his photographs of the Hardenberg Villa and the Neckermann headquarters, a role that had been held by Eberhard Troeger since Berlin times.[64] For health reasons, however, Troeger no longer wanted to accept larger commissions far from his home in Hamburg after 1958, when he had once again worked for Eiermann on a large scale and had recorded the German Pavilion at the Brussels World's Fair for posterity. As with Troeger, after 1960 a friendly relationship was to develop on a private level with Neuendorff, also from Berlin, and his wife, which lasted until the architect's death. Eiermann appreciated the work of Neuendorff, whose black-and-white photography in strong contrasts suited his ideas. Conversely, the photographer quickly understood what the architect wanted. And he was to document all his new works up to the buildings for IBM in Stuttgart and Olivetti in Frankfurt, which were not completed until after his death.

The Neuendorff photographs served Eiermann primarily to ensure that his building was published in trade journals in the way he wanted. He made the photographs, publication plans specially drawn by the office and the text by Brigitte Eiermann, from which we quoted at the beginning, available to all interested editorial offices. Nothing was left to chance. As early as mid-1963, an extensively illustrated article appeared in *Architektur und Wohnform* in his spirit, and after the *Architectural Annual Lotus* published in Milan in 1964 had ranked the Eiermann House in its compilation of the forty most important examples of contemporary residential buildings worldwide, the house was to be illustrated and reviewed in numerous German, English, French and Italian magazines.[65] It probably attracted widespread attention not least because it stood in a certain contrast to the neo-expressive and brutalist currents prevailing in architecture in the 1960s. But even after the house had lost its novelty over the years, its importance as a classic of contemporary architecture was recognised. Wolfgang Pehnt included it in his 1970 compendium *Neue Deutsche Architektur 3* (*New German Architecture 3*), and again and again it was and is presented in interior-design magazines, is the subject of academic publications, in 2002, together with the Hardenberg Villa, it was even the subject of a special exhibition by the Association of German Architects in Baden-Baden, and in 2022 Ulrich Coenen dedicated a 14-part series of articles in the Baden-Baden local press to the Eiermann House, the Hardenberg Villa and the architect's connection with the city. As students of the 1960s report, Eiermann seems to have repeatedly addressed aspects of his domicile in lectures. For them, whose central task in their studies was to design »their own house«, there was great curiosity to learn how their charismatic teacher lived. They virtually made a pilgrimage to Baden-Baden and considered themselves lucky when the opportunity arose to also take a look inside.

The development to this day

Eiermann does not seem to have made much use of his domicile in the seven and a half years that remained until his death. As a busy architect of major projects such as the German Embassy in Washington or the high-rise parliament building in Bonn, as a star of the German architectural scene, as a sought-after prize judge, as a member of commissions and as a university lecturer, he was constantly on the move despite his failing health.[66] When he came home exhausted, he liked to retreat to the studio building, where he usually also slept. He used the large living room almost exclusively for listening to baroque music and jazz on the most modern Braun stereo system of the time. As daughter Anna Eiermann reports, this room, similar to the salon of a 19th century villa, was taboo for her and her schoolmates. However, major social events hardly ever took place in this prestigious ambience. The clavichord, which had been shown in the German section designed by Eiermann at the Triennale in Milan in 1954 and subsequently became his property, was rarely played. When family life took place, it was most likely at the table in the dining room with the hatch to the kitchen. But no paper napkins were allowed there, otherwise Eiermann would immediately start sketching ideas on them and was hardly approachable any more.

The organisation of the house and garden, Brigitte Eiermann's task, proved to be time-consuming. Even the daily watering of the many individual flower pots on the balconies was a challenge in summer, with the water dripping down through the holes in the pots regularly splashing the panes of the windows on the floor below. The drainage of rainwater in the garden also turned out to be a problem. Before they were fixed with concrete, the coarse pebbles in the narrow water channels were washed down the steep slope by the grass with every heavy downpour and had to be laboriously carried back to their place. The placement of the cooker in the kitchen was also less than functional. When frying, fat splashed onto the blind behind it, which was difficult to clean, and which was used to close the hatch. If you opened it to keep it from getting dirty, the kitchen smells would drift unhindered into the dining room. A housekeeper was employed who moved into the separately accessible granny flat on the lower floor, where Eiermann's mother was originally supposed to have moved in. A kind of caretaker came once a week to do rough work in the house and garden. Relatively quickly, serious structural damage became apparent. Contrary to the manufacturer's assurances, the bricks in the area of the terraces and the water basin in the garden – always in areas where soil was behind them – proved to be not frost-proof. The paint did not adhere to the substrate, and parts of the surface of the bricks flaked off. The damage could already not be overlooked in photographs taken in the mid-1960s.

In July 1970, Eiermann suffered another heart attack at the age of only 65. As with the first one in 1960, when he was under great pressure because of the construction of the Memorial Church, it was now the major projects for IBM and Olivetti that put undue strain on him.

Ergebnis gezeigt hatte, zurück nach Hause. Nach seinem Tod wurde es für seine Witwe zunehmend schwieriger, das große Haus für sich und die damals erst 14jährige Tochter zu unterhalten. Nach deren Weggang zum Studium zog Brigitte Eiermann 1976 zurück nach Karlsruhe. Nachdem schon die Einliegerwohnung seit 1971 an einen Musikredakteur des Südwestfunks vermietet worden war, fand sie für das Anwesen mit einem erfolgreichen Medienunternehmer und einer bekannten Schlagersängerin namhafte Mieter. Während die Einbaumöbel bis auf das Regal im Wohnzimmer und einen Wäscheschrank im oberen Flur noch an Ort und Stelle verblieben, nahm Eiermanns Witwe schon damals alle Einzelmöbel mit aus dem Haus. Vieles davon wurde mit den Jahren auf Auktionen versteigert. Das in sich geschlossene Gesamtkunstwerk hatte nicht einmal eineinhalb Jahrzehnte Bestand gehabt.

Eine erste Sanierung des Holzwerks im Äußeren wurde 1983 notwendig. Als die Mieter nach 15 Jahren 1991 auszogen, entschloß sich Brigitte Eiermann schweren Herzens zum Verkauf.[67] Über Anzeigen suchte sie einen Kaufinteressenten, den sie schließlich in Person eines Verlegers einer Büromöbelzeitschrift fand. Die Stadt Baden-Baden, der sie das Haus zuvor angeboten hatte, zeigte sich nicht interessiert.[68] Im Zuge des Verkaufs stufte das Landesdenkmalamt Wohn- und Atelierhaus zusammen mit den Außenanlagen als Kulturdenkmal im Sinne von § 2 des baden-württembergischen Denkmalschutzgesetzes ein. Seit 1999 ist das Anwesen zudem als Kulturdenkmal von besonderer Bedeutung in das Denkmalbuch eingetragen. Dies verhinderte nicht, daß größere Veränderungen stattfanden, die das sensible ästhetische Gefüge teilweise beinträchtigen. Weniger auffällig ist, daß die Sonnensegel aus Leinen durch ein dauerhafteres Kunststoffgewebe ersetzt wurden, die Hanftaue der Befestigung durch Nylonseile. Die meisten Backsteinwände im Inneren erhielten nach und nach unter dem neuen Eigentümer sowie unter dessen Nachfolger, einem durch seine Medienpräsenz in ganz Deutschland bekannt gewordenen Richter am Bundesgerichtshof, einen weißen Anstrich. Es ist durchaus nachvollziehbar, daß nicht jedermann in anthrazitfarbenen Räumen leben möchte, aber natürlich wird dadurch der Zusammenhang von Äußerem und Innerem des Hauses aus dem von Eiermann intendierten Gleichgewicht gebracht. Nachvollziehbar ist auch, daß die offene Gartenloggia unter dem Wohnraum aus wärme- und sicherheitstechnischen Gründen geschlossen wurde. Daß dies mit Fensterelementen aus Aluminium geschah, mag denkmaltheoretischen Grundsätzen der Ablesbarkeit von Veränderungen entsprechen, ästhetisch kann es freilich nicht befriedigen, genausowenig wie die an der Hauptschauseite des Hauses unangenehm ins Auge fallende Leitungsführung der massiven und mit spiegelnder Metallverkleidung versehenen Heizungsrohre vom Haupthaus zum Nebenhaus, welche die alten, unterirdisch verlegten, nur unzureichend gedämmten Rohre abgelöst haben. Der Sichtschutz vor den Fenstern des unteren Geschosses auf der Straßenseite in Form von fassadenbündigen Holzlamellenelementen wurde zugunsten einer Mattverglasung der dahinter liegenden Fenster entfernt. Auch heute noch ist das Haus Ziel von Architekturinteressierten aus aller Welt. Daß diese immer wieder über die neugierig machende, geradezu einladende Treppe mit ihrem Podest neben dem Atelierhaus bis in den völlig offenen Garten vordrangen, war für die Bewohner verständlicherweise kaum erträglich. Der Standardzaun aus Gitterteilen vom Baumarkt, der dies nun seit etlichen Jahren verhindern soll, ist gestalterisch freilich kaum der anspruchsvollen Situation angemessen.

Andere größere Reparaturmaßnahmen, wie der notwendige Ersatz der asbesthaltigen Faserzementplatten des Daches, sind ohne gewichtige ästhetische Einbußen erfolgt. Die seit Jahrzehnten anstehende Grundsanierung des frostgeschädigten Mauerwerks der Terrassenbereiche, zuvor nur mit unzureichenden kosmetischen, ihrerseits nicht dauerhaften Mitteln geflickt, wurde vom letzten Eigentümer und dem sachverständigen Architekten Ulrich Langensteiner aus Ettlingen mit großem Aufwand 2007/08 geplant und ausgeführt. Dabei blieb nichts anderes übrig, als die Bauteile mit soliderem Backsteinmaterial von identischem Aussehen und einer besseren Fundamentierung auszutauschen und auch den Anstrich originalgetreu zu rekonstruieren.[69]

2020 wechselte das Haus abermals den Eigentümer. Die beiden neuen Bewohner, ein Apotheker und ein Tierarzt, haben das Anwesen als Liebhaber moderner Architektur bewußt gegen eine Wohnung in einer historistischen Baden-Badener Villa eingetauscht, die sogar noch etwas mehr Fläche bot. Ihre vor dem Einzug erfolgten umfangreichen Sanierungsmaßnahmen, die von dem Stuttgarter Architekten Karl Amann mit denkmalpflegerischem Fingerspitzengefühl geplant und ausgeführt wurden, zeugen von der Wertschätzung des Eiermannschen Werkes. Der ursprüngliche Raumzuschnitt des Doppelschlafraums von Eiermann und seiner Frau wurde wiederhergestellt, indem die später vermauerte Öffnung geöffnet wurde. Die gesamte Elektrik wurde erneuert, wobei sich die alten Leerrohre bewährt haben, in die neue Kabel eingezogen werden konnten. Das originale Bild der Schalter und Steckdosen wurde gewahrt, da diese bis heute noch lieferbar sind, wenn auch mit neuem technischen Innenleben. Nach einer detaillierten Befunduntersuchung und -dokumentation durch eine kompetente Restauratorin wurde das gesamte Holzwerk im Innern aufgearbeitet. Die Einbauküchen im Haupt- und Nebenhaus sind als originale Ausstattungsteile der Erbauungszeit vor Ort erhalten, die Arbeitsplatte in der Hauptküche wurde in ihrer ursprünglichen Optik als weiße Fläche nachgebildet. Die Garderobe, bei der Eiermann, typisch für sein Design, die Hutablage in Metallkonstruktion mit Korbwerk beflechten ließ, ist unverändert geblieben. Die durch den langen Gebrauch nachgedunkelten und stumpf gewordenen Fliesenböden wurden durch eine schonende Grundreinigung wieder zum farbenfreudigen Leuchten gebracht. In den Bädern passen sich neue Elemente, speziell die runden Waschbecken und die ebenfalls runden Spiegel, sehr geglückt dem Bestehenden an. Für den oberen Flur und das Schlafzimmer sind nach Entwürfen von Karl Amann eigens Schränke angefertigt worden, die mit den Materialien Holz und Melaminharz die Optik der verlorenen Einbaumöbel von Eiermann aufnehmen, aber auch den Bedürfnissen der heutigen Nutzer entsprechen. An die Stelle der Einzelmöbel Eiermanns sind Möbelklassiker des 20. Jahrhunderts von Charles Eames, Le Corbusier und Fritz Haller getreten, die neue Akzente setzen, dem Haus aber seine individuelle Eigenart belassen.

He died in the back seat of his car on the autobahn, his wife just driving him back to his home from a routine check-up at the hospital, which had actually shown a favourable result. After his death, it became increasingly difficult for his widow to maintain the large building for herself and their daughter, who was only 14 at the time. After her daughter left to study, Brigitte Eiermann moved back to Karlsruhe in 1976. After the granny flat had been rented to a music editor of the Südwestfunk radio station since 1971, she found well-known tenants for the property in a successful media entrepreneur and a well-known pop singer. While the built-in furniture remained in place except for the shelf in the living room and a linen cupboard in the upstairs hallway, Eiermann's widow took all the individual pieces of furniture out of the house even then. Much of it was sold at auctions over the years. The self-contained *Gesamtkunstwerk* had not even lasted a dec-ade and a half.

A first renovation of the wooden exterior became necessary in 1983. When the tenants moved out after 15 years in 1991, Brigitte Eiermann decided with a heavy heart to sell.[67] Through advertisements she looked for a prospective buyer, whom she finally found in the person of a publisher of an office furniture magazine. The city of Baden-Baden, to whom she had previously offered the house, showed no interest.[68] In the course of the sale, the State Office for the Protection of Monuments classified the residential and studio building together with the outdoor facilities as a cultural monument in the sense of § 2 of the Baden-Württemberg Monument Protection Act. Since 1999, the property has also been entered in the register of monuments as a cultural monument of special importance. This has not prevented major alterations from taking place, some of which have affected the sensitive aesthetic structure. Less noticeably, the canvas awnings have been replaced by a more durable synthetic fabric, and the hemp ropes used to fasten them have been replaced by nylon ropes. Most of the brick walls inside were gradually given a coat of white paint under the new owner and under his successor, a judge at the Federal Court of Justice who has become famous throughout Germany for his media presence. It is quite understandable that not everyone wants to live in anthracite-coloured rooms, but of course this throws the relationship between the exterior and interior of the house out of the balance intended by Eiermann. It is also understandable that the open garden loggia under the living room was closed off for reasons of warmth and safety. The fact that this was done with window elements made of aluminium may correspond to the theoretical principles of the preservation of historic monuments, but aesthetically it is not satisfactory, just as little as the unpleasantly eye-catching routing of the massive heating pipes with reflective metal cladding from the main building to the studio building, which have replaced the old, insufficiently insulated pipes that were laid underground. The privacy screen in front of the windows of the lower storey on the street side in the form of wooden slat elements flush with the façade was removed in favour of frosted glazing for the windows behind. Even today, the house is a destination for architecture enthusiasts from all over the world. Understandably, the residents found it almost unbearable that these visitors repeatedly penetrated the completely open garden via the curiously inviting staircase with its landing next to the studio building. The standard fence made of lattice parts from the construction market, which has now been preventing this for several years, is admittedly hardly appropriate to the demanding situation in terms of design.

Other major repair measures, such as the necessary replacement of the asbestos-containing corrugated fibre-cement panels on the roof, have been carried out without any significant aesthetic loss. The basic renovation of the frost-damaged masonry of the terrace areas, which had been pending for decades and had previously only been patched up with inadequate cosmetic measures that were themselves not durable, was planned and carried out at great expense in 2007/08 by the last owner and the expert architect Ulrich Langensteiner from Ettlingen. There was nothing else to do but to replace the structural elements with more solid brick material of identical appearance and better foundation, and also to reconstruct the painting true to the original.[69]

In 2020, the house changed hands again. The two new residents, a pharmacist and a veterinarian, as lovers of modern architecture, deliberately exchanged a flat in a historic Baden-Baden villa, one that even offered a little more space, for the Eiermann property. Their extensive renovations before moving in, which were planned and executed by the Stuttgart architect Karl Amann with a flair for the preservation of historical monuments, bear witness to their appreciation of Eiermann's work. The original room layout of the double bedroom of Eiermann and his wife was restored by opening the aperture that was later bricked up. The entire electrical system was renewed, with the old empty conduits – into which new cables could be pulled – proving their worth. The original appearance of the switches and sockets was preserved, as these are still available today, albeit with a new technical interior. After a detailed examination and documentation of the findings by a competent restorer, the entire interior woodwork was refurbished. The fitted kitchens in the main and side buildings have been preserved on site as original fittings from the time of construction, and the worktop in the main kitchen has been recreated in its original appearance as a white surface. The wardrobe, where Eiermann, typical of his design, had the hat shelf woven in metal construction with basketwork, has remained unchanged. The tiled floors, darkened and dulled by long use, were restored to their colourful glow by a gentle basic cleaning. In the bathrooms, new elements, especially the round washbasins and the mirrors, which are also round, fit in very well with the existing ones. For the upper hallway and the bedroom, cabinets have been specially made according to designs by Karl Amann. Using wood and melamine resin, they take up the look of Eiermann's lost built-in furniture, but also meet the needs of today's users. Eiermann's individual pieces of furniture have been replaced by 20th-century furniture classics by Charles Eames, Le Corbusier and Fritz Haller, which set new accents but leave the house with its individual character.

Anmerkungen

[1] *Architektur und Wohnform. Innendekoration*, 71. Jg., H. 7, Oktober 1963, S. 302.
[2] Vorlesung »Über die Wahrheit in der Architektur« aus dem Jahr 1963, Tondokument im Eiermann-Nachlaß des saai | Archiv für Architektur und Ingenieurbau am Karlsruher Institut für Technologie. Umschrift in *Egon Eiermann (1904–1970). Zwei Wohnhäuser in Baden-Baden. Ein Stück deutsche Architekturgeschichte*, Ausstellungskatalog, BDA Baden-Baden 2002, S. 26.
[3] Baubeschreibung von 1962/63 zur Erläuterung der Photos des Neubaus von Horstheinz Neuendorff für die Publikation in Bauzeitschriften, saai, Werkarchiv Egon Eiermann, Haus Eiermann, Bauakten.
[4] *Architektur und Wohnform. Innendekoration*, 71. Jg., H. 7, Oktober 1963, S. 293.
[5] *Architektur und Wohnform. Innendekoration*, 71. Jg., H. 7, Oktober 1963, S. 292.
[6] Zum Beispiel als Titel der Publikation in *Architektur und Wohnform. Innendekoration*, 71. Jg., H. 7, Oktober 1963.
[7] Im Sinne von Le Corbusiers Formulierung im Hinblick auf seine Villenbauten der 1920er Jahre.
[8] Die mächtige Baumwurzel stammte von der weiträumigen Rodung des Rheinauewaldes auf der Großbaustelle der DEA-Scholven-Ölraffinerie in Karlsruhe, wo Eiermann Anfang der 1960er Jahre die Errichtung einer Vielzahl von Funktionsgebäuden übertragen worden war.
[9] Nach Aussage von ehemaligen Studenten von Eiermann brachte dieser das Thema des Schwitzwassers in Garagen häufig in seinen Vorlesungen.
[10] Vgl. Robert Venturi, *Komplexität und Widerspruch in der Architektur*, Braunschweig 1978. Amerikanische Erstausgabe: *Complexity and Contradiction in Architecture*, Museum of Modern Art, New York 1966).
[11] saai, Werkarchiv Egon Eiermann, Haus Eiermann, Baden-Baden, Skizzen.
[12] Zum frühen Schaffen Eiermanns vgl. Sonja Hildebrand, *Egon Eiermann. Die Berliner Zeit. Das architektonische Gesamtwerk bis 1945*, Braunschweig/Wiesbaden 1999.
[13] Zum Haus Hesse vgl. Hildebrand 1999 (wie Anm. 12), S. 54–58.
[14] Wie der Briefwechsel im Werkarchiv Eiermann dokumentiert, bestand noch in den 1960er Jahren der Kontakt zwischen der Tochter von Behrens und Eiermann.
[15] Vgl. Annemarie Jaeggi (Hg.), *Egon Eiermann (1904 bis 1970). Die Kontinuität der Moderne*, Ausstellungskatalog, Karlsruhe / Berlin 2004, S. 12.
[16] Sonja Hildebrand hat Eiermanns Verhalten im »Dritten Reich« gründlich aufgearbeitet. Einerseits räumt sie auf mit dem Bild eines Widerständlers Eiermann, wie es von Schülern der Nachkriegszeit gerne gesehen wurde, andererseits relativiert sie die Vermutung einer tiefen Verstrickung mit dem NS-Staat. Man kann ihm allenfalls vorwerfen, daß er für die Sicherung seines Büros und die Freistellung vom Kriegsdienst Aufträge übernahm, die der Kriegswirtschaft diente. Selbst die von ihm errichtete Feuerlöscherfabrik Total in Apolda bediente nicht nur friedliche Zwecke, sondern produzierte auch Flammenwerfer für das deutsche Militär.
[17] Zu Eiermanns beiden Räumen auf der Ausstellung vgl. Hildebrand 1999 (wie Anm. 12), S. 138–148.
[18] Zur Kaserne in Rathenow vgl. Hildebrand 1999 (wie Anm. 12), S. 148–152.
[19] Vgl. Herta Steingroever, *Mein Leben im Eiermann-Haus. Vom Haus und seinen Bewohnern*, Berlin 2022.
[20] Zum Haus Vollberg vgl. Hildebrand 1999 (wie Anm. 12), S. 102–117.
[21] Zum Ausweichkrankenhaus vgl. Hildebrand (wie Anm. 12 20), S. 214–226.
[22] Zum Beelitzer Holzhaus vgl. Hildebrand (wie Anm. 12), S. 226–230.
[23] Vgl. *Das Eiermann-Magnani-Haus*, Katalog zur Ausstellung in Hettingen, Wüstenrot Stiftung und Haus der Geschichte Baden-Württemberg, Ludwigsburg/Stuttgart 2018.
[24] Vgl. Wulf Schirmer (Hg.), *Egon Eiermann 1904–1970. Bauten und Projekte*, Stuttgart 1984. – Annemarie Jaeggi (Hg.), *Egon Eiermann (1904 bis 1970). Die Kontinuität der Moderne*, Ausstellungskatalog, Karlsruhe / Berlin 2004.
[25] Planunterlagen zu den Häusern Klein und Feith im Werkarchiv Eiermann des saai.
[26] Vgl. Egon Eiermann 1984 (wie Anm. 24), S. 172–175. – *Egon Eiermann (1904–1970). Zwei Wohnhäuser in Baden-Baden. Ein Stück deutsche Architekturgeschichte*, Ausstellungskatalog, BDA Baden-Baden 2002.
[27] Vgl. *Bunte Illustrierte*, H. 35, 31.06.1957, S. 38/39.
[28] *Egon Eiermann. Briefe des Architekten 1946–1970*, Stuttgart 1994, S. 110.
[29] Vgl. *Rudolf Büchner. Arbeiten aus der Praxis 1941 bis 1983*, Ausstellungskatalog, Architektursammlung des Instituts für Baugeschichte an der Universität Karlsruhe 1988, S. 56–57.
[30] saai, Werkarchiv Egon Eiermann, Haus Eiermann, Baden-Baden, Schreiben vom 12.7.1962.
[31] Vgl. Hildebrand 1999 (wie Anm. 12), S. 88–91, 102–105.
[32] Es handelte sich offensichtlich um einen Vorvertrag. Die Zahlung des Kaufpreises an die Stadt erfolgte laut einer Aufstellung der Kosten in den Bauakte des Hauses im Eiermann-Nachlaß des saai erst am 12.11.1959.
[33] Karin Kirsch ist im gründlich recherchierten Beitrag zum Eiermann Haus in ihrem Buch *Die neue Wohnung und das alte Japan. Architekten planen für sich selbst*, Stuttgart 1996, S.158–182, bereits ausführlich auf die Planungsgeschichte des Hauses Eiermann eingegangen. Offensichtlich waren ihr jedoch die beiden Alternativentwürfe der ersten Planungsphase von Ende 1958 nicht bekannt. Pläne und Bauakten im saai.
[34] Vgl. Egon Eiermann 1984 (wie Anm. 24), S. 308.
[35] Persönliche Gespräche des Autors mit der 2018 verstorbenen Brigitte Eiermann sowie Aussagen im 2002 für die Baden-Badener Ausstellung »Zwei Wohnhäuser in Baden-Baden. Ein Stück Deutsche Architekturgeschichte« aufgenommenen Interview mit ihr; dieses digitalisiert im saai, Werkarchiv Egon Eiermann.
[36] saai, Werkarchiv Egon Eiermann, Haus Eiermann, Baden-Baden, Bauakten, Baugenehmigung vom 26.10.1959.
[37] saai, Werkarchiv Egon Eiermann, Haus Eiermann, Baden-Baden, Bauakten, Brief vom 4.11.1960.
[38] Ich danke Kurt Huppert, Frankfurt am Main, für telephonische Auskünfte über seine Tätigkeit im Büro Eiermann und als Bauleiter beim Baden-Badener Haus.
[39] Das weißgestrichene Wasserrohr zur Berieselung ist heute leider nicht mehr vorhanden. Auf historischen Photographien ist es aber gut zu erkennen. Heute sieht man nur noch den Ansatz des Rohres an den beiden Giebelwänden.
[40] saai, Werkarchiv Egon Eiermann, Haus Eiermann, Baden-Baden, Bauakten, Schreiben vom 09.08.1961. Weitere Schreiben Eiermanns in der Angelegenheit in derselben Akte.
[41] saai, Werkarchiv Egon Eiermann, Haus Eiermann, Baden-Baden, Schreiben vom 17.03.1961.
[42] saai, Werkarchiv Egon Eiermann, Haus Eiermann, Baden-Baden, Bauakten, Schreiben vom 27.06.1962.
[43] saai, Werkarchiv Egon Eiermann, Haus Eiermann, Baden-Baden, Bauakte, Schreiben vom 25.06.1962.
[44] saai, Werkarchiv Egon Eiermann, Haus Eiermann, Baden-Baden, Bauakten, Schreiben vom 06.07.1961.
[45] saai, Werkarchiv Egon Eiermann, Haus Eiermann, Baden-Baden, Bauakten, Schreiben an den Baden-Badener Oberbürgermeister Schlapper vom 12.07.1962.
[46] saai, Werkarchiv Egon Eiermann, Haus Eiermann, Baden-Baden, Bauakten, Schreiben vom 12.07.1962.
[47] saai, Werkarchiv Egon Eiermann, Haus Eiermann, Baden-Baden, Bauakten, Schreiben vom 12.08.1966.
[48] In Vorlesungen kritisierte er nach Aussagen von Studenten immer wieder vor allem Le Corbusiers spätere Bauten als subjektiv, als gebaute Plastiken, die nichts mit wahrer Architektur zu tun hätten. Die Wallfahrtskirche in Ronchamp war bald nach ihrer Fertigstellung Mitte der 1950er Jahre eigens Ziel einer Exkursion der Karlsruher Architekturfakultät unter Leitung von Eiermann und Rudolf Büchner. Nach Aussage des inzwischen verstorbenen Eiermann-Schülers Heinrich Stephan fand Eiermann dort kein gutes Wort für Le Corbusiers spektakuläre Architektur. Die Kapelle sei eine begehbare Plastik wie die Freiheitsstatue in New York, damit blanker Kitsch, die Konstruktion der Fensterwand mit Spritzbeton auf Maschendraht gaukele Massivität vor, die in Wirklichkeit nicht existiere.
[49] Vielleicht gab dazu Walter Gropius' Raumdisposition seines Hauses in Lincoln bei Boston von 1938 eine gewisse Anregung. Eiermann hatte Gropius bei seinen USA-Reisen 1950 und 1956 dort besucht. Veranda und Terrassen sind vor den Wohnräumen ebenso als direkte Verlängerung der Innenräume interpretiert.
[50] saai, Werkarchiv Egon Eiermann, Haus Eiermann, Baden-Baden, Bauakten, Schreiben vom 23.05.1962.
[51] Ich danke Andreas Eiermann, Baden-Baden, für den Hinweis, daß er den Holzstoß mehrfach neu aufsetzen mußte, bis sein Vater mit der Verteilung der verschiedenen Durchmesser der Rundhölzer in der Fläche zufrieden war. Das Holz sei nie als Feuerholz für den Kamin verwendet worden, sondern diente rein dekorativen Zwecken.
[52] Zu Eiermann als Möbelgestalter vgl. *Egon Eiermann. Die Möbel*, Ausstellungskatalog, Badisches Landesmuseum, Karlsruhe 1999.
[53] Es haben sich noch Dutzende von Skizzen und Werkplänen im Werkarchiv Eiermann des saai erhalten.
[54] saai, Werkarchiv Eiermann, Haus Eiermann Baden-Baden, Bauakten. Schreiben vom 07.11.1962.
[55] Siehe das Literaturverzeichnis zum Haus Eiermann, S. 40.
[56] saai, Werkarchiv Egon Eiermann, Haus Eiermann, Baden-Baden, Bauakten, Schreiben vom 27.06.1962.
[57] saai, Werkarchiv Egon Eiermann, Haus Eiermann, Baden-Baden, Bauakten, Schreiben vom 06.07.1961.
[58] Tetsuro Yoshida, *Das Japanische Wohnhaus*, Berlin 1935; 2. Aufl. Tübingen 1954.
[59] saai, Werkarchiv Egon Eiermann, Akten Lehre.
[60] Ich danke Anna Eiermann, Berlin, für diesen Hinweis. Japan kennenzulernen, war auch für Brigitte Eiermann ein solches Bedürfnis, daß sie nach Eiermanns Tod Mitte der 1970er Jahre tatsächlich mit ihrer Tochter dorthin eine Studienreise unternahm.
[61] Hinweis von Anna Eiermann, Berlin.

Notes

[1] *Architektur und Wohnform. Innendekoration*, 71st. vol., no. 7, October 1963, p. 302.
[2] Vorlesung »Über die Wahrheit in der Architektur« aus dem Jahr 1963, audio document in the Eiermann estate of the saai | Archiv für Architektur und Ingenieurbau am Karlsruher Institut für Technologie. Transcription in *Egon Eiermann (1904–1970). Zwei Wohnhäuser in Baden-Baden. Ein Stück deutsche Architekturgeschichte*, exhibition catalogue, BDA Baden-Baden 2002, p. 26.
[3] Building description from 1962/63 explaining the photographs of the new building by Horstheinz Neuendorff for publication in building journals, saai, work archive Egon Eiermann, Eiermann House, building files.
[4] *Architektur und Wohnform. Innendekoration*, 71st vol., no. 7, October 1963, p. 293.
[5] *Architektur und Wohnform. Innendekoration*, 71st vol., no. 7, October 1963, p. 292.
[6] For example, as the title of the publication in *Architektur und Wohnform. Innendekoration*, 71st vol., no. 7, October 1963.
[7] In the sense of Le Corbusier's formulation with regard to his villa buildings of the 1920s.
[8] The mighty tree root came from the extensive clearing of the Rheinauewald on the large construction site of the DEA-Scholven oil refinery in Karlsruhe, where Eiermann had been entrusted with the construction of a large number of functional buildings in the early 1960s.
[9] According to former students of Eiermann, he frequently brought up the subject of condensation in garages in his lectures.
[10] Vgl. Robert Venturi, *Komplexität und Widerspruch in der Architektur*, Braunschweig 1978. First American edition: *Complexity and Contradiction in Architecture*, Museum of Modern Art, New York 1966).
[11] saai, work archive Egon Eiermann, Eiermann House, Baden-Baden, sketches.
[12] On Eiermann's early work cf. Sonja Hildebrand, *Egon Eiermann. Die Berliner Zeit. Das architektonische Gesamtwerk bis 1945*, Braunschweig/Wiesbaden 1999.
[13] On the Hesse House cf. Hildebrand 1999 (like note 12), pp. 54–58.
[14] As the correspondence in the Eiermann work archive documents, Behrens' daughter and Eiermann were still in contact in the 1960s.
[15] Cf. Annemarie Jaeggi (ed.), *Egon Eiermann (1904 bis 1970). Die Kontinuität der Moderne*, Exhibition catalogue, Karlsruhe / Berlin 2004, p. 12.
[16] Sonja Hildebrand has thoroughly explored Eiermann's behaviour in the »Third Reich«. On the one hand, she cleared up the image of Eiermann as a resister, as students of the post-war period would have liked to see it, and on the other hand, she relativised the assumption of a deep involvement with the Nazi state. At most, he could be accused of taking on commissions that served the war economy in order to secure his office and exemption from military service. Even the Total fire extinguisher factory he built in Apolda not only served peaceful purposes, but also produced flamethrowers for the German military.
[17] On Eiermann's two rooms at the exhibition cf. Hildebrand 1999 (like note 12), pp. 138–148.
[18] On the barracks in Rathenow cf. Hildebrand 1999 (like note 12), pp. 148–152.
[19] Cf. Herta Steingroever, *Mein Leben im Eiermann-Haus. Vom Haus und seinen Bewohnern*, Berlin 2022.
[20] On the Vollberg House cf. Hildebrand 1999 (like note 12), pp. 102–117.
[21] On the alternative hospital cf. Hildebrand (like note 12), pp. 214–226.
[22] On the Beelitz wooden house cf. Hildebrand (like note 12), pp. 226–230.
[23] Vgl. *Das Eiermann-Magnani-Haus*, catalogue for the exhibition in Hettingen, Wüstenrot Stiftung and Haus der Geschichte Baden-Württemberg, Ludwigsburg / Stuttgart 2018.
[24] Vgl. Wulf Schirmer (ed.), *Egon Eiermann 1904–1970. Bauten und Projekte*, Stuttgart 1984. – Annemarie Jaeggi (ed.), *Egon Eiermann (1904 bis 1970). Die Kontinuität der Moderne*, exhibition catalogue, Karlsruhe / Berlin 2004.
[25] Planning documents for the Klein and Feith Houses in the work archive Eiermann of the saai.
[26] Cf. Egon Eiermann 1984 (like note 24), pp. 172–175. – *Egon Eiermann (1904–1970). Zwei Wohnhäuser in Baden-Baden. Ein Stück deutsche Architekturgeschichte*, exhibition catalogue, BDA Baden-Baden 2002.
[27] Vgl. *Bunte Illustrierte*, no. 35, 31.06.1957, pp. 38/39.
[28] *Egon Eiermann. Briefe des Architekten 1946–1970*, Stuttgart 1994, p. 110.
[29] Vgl. *Rudolf Büchner. Arbeiten aus der Praxis 1941 bis 1983*, exhibition catalogue, Architektursammlung des Instituts für Baugeschichte an der Universität Karlsruhe 1988, pp. 56–57.
[30] saai, work archive Egon Eiermann, Eiermann House, Baden-Baden, writing from 12.7.1962.
[31] Cf. Hildebrand 1999 (like note 12), pp. 88–91, 102–105.
[32] This was obviously a preliminary contract. According to a list of costs in the building file of the house in the Eiermann archive of the saai, payment of the purchase price to the city did not take place until 12.11.1959.
[33] Karin Kirsch has already gone into the planning history of the Eiermann House in detail in her book *Die neue Wohnung und das alte Japan. Architekten planen für sich selbst*, Stuttgart 1996, pp.158–182. Obviously, however, she was not aware of the two alternative designs from the first planning phase at the end of 1958. Plans and building files in the saai.
[34] Cf. Egon Eiermann 1984 (like note 24), p. 308.
[35] Personal conversations of the author with Brigitte Eiermann, who died in 2018, as well as statements in an interview with her for the 2002 exhibition »Zwei Wohnhäuser in Baden-Baden. A Piece of German Architectural History«; this interview is digitically stored in the work archive Egon Eiermann of the saai.
[36] saai, work archive Egon Eiermann, Eiermann House, Baden-Baden, building files, building permission from 26.10.1959.
[37] saai, work archive Egon Eiermann, Eiermann House, Baden-Baden, building files, letter from 4.11.1960.
[38] I would like to thank Kurt Huppert, Frankfurt am Main, for information by telephone about his work in the Eiermann office and as site manager at the Baden-Baden house.
[39] Unfortunately, the white-painted water pipe for sprinkling no longer exists today. However, it is clearly visible in historical photographs. Today, only the base of the pipe can be seen on the two gable walls.
[40] saai, work archive Egon Eiermann, Eiermann House, Baden-Baden, building files, writing from 09.08.1961. Further letters by Eiermann on the matter in the same file.
[41] saai, work archive Egon Eiermann, Eiermann House, Baden-Baden, writing from 17.03.1961.
[42] saai, work archive Egon Eiermann, Eiermann House, Baden-Baden, building files, writing from 27.06.1962.
[43] saai, work archive Egon Eiermann, Eiermann House, Baden-Baden, Bauakte, writing from 25.06.1962.
[44] saai, work archive Egon Eiermann, Eiermann House, Baden-Baden, building files, writing from 06.07.1961.
[45] saai, work archive Egon Eiermann, Eiermann House, Baden-Baden, building files, letter to the mayor of Baden-Baden Schlapper from 12.07.1962.
[46] saai, work archive Egon Eiermann, Eiermann House, Baden-Baden, building files, writing from 12.07.1962.
[47] saai, work archive Egon Eiermann, Eiermann House, Baden-Baden, building files, writing from 12.08.1966.
[48] In lectures, according to students, he repeatedly criticised Le Corbusier's later buildings in particular as subjective, as built sculptures that had nothing to do with true architecture. Soon after its completion in the mid-1950s, the pilgrimage church in Ronchamp was the special destination of an excursion by the Karlsruhe architecture faculty led by Eiermann and Rudolf Büchner. According to the now deceased Eiermann student Heinrich Stephan, Eiermann did not find a good word there for Le Corbusier's spectacular architecture. The chapel, he said, was a walk-in sculpture like the Statue of Liberty in New York, and thus sheer kitsch; the construction of the window wall with sprayed concrete on wire mesh simulated solidity that did not exist in reality.
[49] Perhaps Walter Gropius' room disposition of his house in Lincoln near Boston in 1938 provided some inspiration for this. Eiermann had visited Gropius there during his trips to the USA in 1950 and 1956. The veranda and terraces in front of the living rooms are also interpreted as direct extensions of the interior spaces.
[50] saai, work archive Egon Eiermann, Eiermann House, Baden-Baden, building files, writing from 23.05.1962.
[51] I am grateful to Andreas Eiermann, Baden-Baden, for pointing out that he had to reposition the woodpile several times until his father was satisfied with the distribution of the various diameters of the round logs in the area. The wood had never been used as firewood for the fireplace, but served purely decorative purposes.
[52] On Eiermann as a furniture designer cf. *Egon Eiermann. Die Möbel*, exhibition catalogue, Badisches Landesmuseum, Karlsruhe 1999.
[53] Dozens of sketches and work plans have been preserved in the work archive Eiermann of the saai.
[54] saai, work archive Eiermann, Eiermann House Baden-Baden, building files, writing from 07.11.1962.
[55] See the publication list on the Eiermann House, p. 41.
[56] saai, work archive Egon Eiermann, Eiermann House, Baden-Baden, building files, writing from 27.06.1962.
[57] saai, work archive Egon Eiermann, Eiermann House, Baden-Baden, building files, writing from 06.07.1961.
[58] Tetsuro Yoshida, *Das Japanische Wohnhaus*, Berlin 1935; 2nd ed. Tübingen 1954.
[59] saai, work archive Egon Eiermann, Akten Lehre.
[60] I would like to thank Anna Eiermann, Berlin, for this reference. Brigitte Eiermann also felt such a need to get to know Japan that after Eiermann's death in the mid-1970s she actually went there with her daughter on a study trip.
[61] Note from Anna Eiermann, Berlin.
[62] Note from Brigitte Eiermann, Karlsruhe, who died in 2018.

[62] Hinweis der 2018 verstorbenen Brigitte Eiermann, Karlsruhe.
[63] Ein Schreiben des Vaters an den Sohn wegen der Überlassung des Bootes im saai, Werkarchiv Egon Eiermann, Briefe.
[64] Glasplattennegative und eine Vielzahl von Papierabzügen der Photos des Baden-Badener Hauses von Neuendorff (1925–2016) befinden sich im Werkarchiv Eiermann des saai. Eiermann und Troeger (1905–1964) hatten sich im Berlin der 1930er Jahre kennengelernt. Auch die große Distanz, die nach dem Krieg entstanden war, weil es Troeger nach Hamburg, Eiermann nach Karlsruhe verschlagen hatte, verhinderte in der Nachkriegszeit nicht, daß Eiermann vornehmlich Troeger für Photoaufträge heranzog.
[65] Zu den Publikationen siehe das Literaturverzeichnis zum Haus Eiermann, S. 40.
[66] Die folgenden Informationen verdanke ich Gesprächen mit der 2018 verstorbenen Brigitte Eiermann in Karlsruhe, Anna Eiermann in Berlin und Andreas Eiermann in Baden-Baden.
[67] saai, Werkarchiv Egon Eiermann, Haus Eiermann, Baden-Baden, Akten nach 1970.
[66] Der Wert war intern von der Stadt mit rund zwei Millionen Mark eingeschätzt worden.
[69] Die Mauerwerksschäden zeigen sich gegenwärtig noch am völlig maroden Tauchbecken im Garten, das mit Kies aufgefüllt ist, sowie an den Mauern des in den Hang eingeschnittenen Wäschetrockenplatzes östlich neben dem Haus. Beide für die Gesamtanlage des Anwesens wichtigen Bauelemente sind 2023 noch nicht restauriert.

Veröffentlichungen zum Haus Eiermann (Auswahl)

Brigitte Eiermann, »Egon Eiermann, Haus und Nebenhaus in Baden-Baden«, *Architektur und Wohnform, Innendekoration*, 71. Jg., 1963, H. 7, S. 291–307.

»Einfamiliehus in Baden-Baden«, *Architekten*, 1964, Nr. 16, S. 330 ff.

Guilia Veronei, Bruno Alfieri, *Lotus. Architectural annual 1964–1965*, Mailand 1964, S. 206 ff.

»Una casa per ciascuno«, *L'architettura*, 10. Jg., 1964, S. 182 f.

Eberhard Schulz, »Das eigene Haus des Architekten«, *Frankfurter Allgemeine Zeitung*, 13.06.1964.

Eberhard Schulz, »Das eigene Haus des Architekten«. *Die Prediger mit dem Reißbrett*, Stuttgart 1964, S. 31 ff.

Heinz W. Krewinkel, »Haus und Nebenhaus in Baden-Baden. Architekt: Prof. Egon Eiermann«, *Glasforum*, 1964, H. 2, S. 4–9.

»Allemagne. Maison de l'architecte à Baden-Baden«, *Technique & Architecture*, 26. Jg., 1965, Nr. 2, S. 152 ff.

»Egon Eiermann. Das Detail ist das einzig Noble«, *Schöner Wohnen*, 1965, H. 7, S. 58–65.

»Baden-Baden. An architect's home and guest house. Maison d'un architecte avec dépendance. Haus eines Architekten«, *ac, Revue internationale d'amiante-ciment. Internationale Asbestzement-Revue. International asbestos-cement review*, Nr. 43, 1966, H. 3, S. 28–31.

H. O. Eckhardt, »Woonhuizen in Baden-Baden, architect: Prof. E. Eiermann«, *Bouw*, 1966, Nr. 26, S. 1010/1011.

»Habitations à Baden-Baden. Egon Eiermann, architecte«, *L'Architecture d'Aujourd'hui*, 36. Jg., 1966, Nr. 124, S. 63.

»Eiermann's Own«, *The Architectural Review*, 1966, Nr. 838, S. 392 f.

»Architektenhaus in Baden-Baden«, in: Werner Weidert, *Einfamilienhäuser international*, Stuttgart 1967, S. 68 ff.

Wend Fischer, *Geborgenheit und Freiheit. Vom Bauen mit Glas*, Krefeld 1970, S. 300 ff.

»Haus Eiermann in Baden-Baden. 1960, 1961–62«, in: Wolfgang Pehnt, *Neue deutsche Architektur 3*, Stuttgart 1970, S. 46 ff.

»Egon Eiermann, Eiermann House« in: Yukio Futagawa, *Global Interior 3. Houses in Northern Europe*, Tokio 1972, S. 136 ff.

Wulf Schirmer (Hg.), *Egon Eiermann 1904–1970. Bauten und Projekte*, Stuttgart 1984, S. 186–189.

Lore Kelly, »Filigrane Leichtigkeit«. in: *Raum und Wohnen. Schweizer Magazin für Architektur, Wohnen und Design*, 1993, Nr. 2, S. 38–48.

Lore Kelly, »Radikal modern«, in: *Wohndesign. Internationales Magazin für Architektur, Wohnen und Design*, 1993, H. 4, S. 59–66.

Karin Kirsch, »Egon Eiermann, Wohnhaus und Atelier in Baden-Baden«, in: *Die neue Wohnung und das alte Japan. Architekten planen für sich selbst*, Stuttgart 1996, S. 160–181.

Friedrich Grimm / Clemens Richarz, *Gestalten mit der Welle*, Stuttgart / Zürich 1998, S. 32–37.

Günter Mader, »Ein Garten von Egon Eiermann«. in: *Gartenkunst des 20. Jahrhunderts. Garten und Landschaftsarchitektur in Deutschland*, Stuttgart 1999, S. 138–141.

Clemens Kieser, »›Ich wollte kein Wohnhaus mehr bauen‹. Die Villenbauten Egon Eiermanns in Baden-Baden«, *Denkmalpflege in Baden-Württemberg, Nachrichtenblatt des Landesdenkmalamtes*, Bd. 29, 2000, H. 4, S. 254–260.

Brigitte Eiermann, »Wohnhaus Eiermann, Baden-Baden, Krippenhof«, in: *Egon Eiermann, Bauten in Baden-Württemberg 1946–1972*, hg. von der Egon-Eiermann-Gesellschaft e.V., o. O., 2000, S. 92–99.

Peter Krebs, »Wohnhaus Eiermann, Egon Eiermann (1904–1970)«, *Baumeister*, 98. Jg., 2001, H. 4, S. 72–77.

Egon Eiermann (1904–1970). Zwei Wohnhäuser in Baden-Baden. Ein Stück Deutsche Architekturgeschichte, Bund Deutscher Architekten BDA, Kreisgruppe Baden-Baden, Rastatt, Ortenau, Baden-Baden 2002.

Clemens Kieser, »Wohnhaus Eiermann Baden-Baden, 1959–1962«, in: *Egon Eiermann 1904–1970. Die Kontinuität der Moderne*, Ausstellungskatalog, Städtische Galerie Karlsruhe, Bauhaus-Archiv, Berlin, 2004/2005, S. 194–197.

Gennaro Postiglione (Hg.), *Hundert Häuser für hundert europäische Architekten des zwanzigsten Jahrhunderts*, Köln / London / Los Angeles / Madrid / Paris / Tokyo 2004, S. 94–99.

Ulrich Coenen, Zeitungsartikel zu Egon Eiermann und seinen Häusern in Baden und der Sanierung des Hauses Eiermann, *Badisches Tagblatt*, Baden-Baden, 10.2.2021, 11.9.2021, 5.1.2022, 13.1.2022, 14.1.2022, 18.1.2022, 20.1.2022, 25.1.2022, 27.1.2022, 3.2.2022, 8.2.2022, 9.2.2022, 11.2.2022, 12.2.2022, 14.2.2022, 2.8.2023.
(Der Inhalt der Artikel erscheint vor Ende 2023 als Publikation im Verlag Mainz in Aachen unter dem Titel *Egon Eiermann in Mittelbaden – Anmerkungen zu seinen Villen in Baden-Baden und seinen Gewerbebauten in Offenburg*).

[63] A letter from the father to the son concerning the transfer of the boat in the saai, work archive Egon Eiermann, letters.
[64] Glass plate negatives and a large number of paper prints of photographs of the house in Baden-Baden by Neuendorff (1925–2016) are in the work archive Eiermann of the saai. Eiermann and Troeger (1905-1964) had met in Berlin in the 1930s. Even the great distance that had arisen after the war, because Troeger had moved to Hamburg and Eiermann to Karlsruhe, did not prevent Eiermann from mainly using Troeger for photographic commissions in the post-war period
[65] For publications see the bibliography concerning the Eiermann House, p. 41.
[66] I owe the following information to conversations with Brigitte Eiermann in Karlsruhe, who died in 2018, Anna Eiermann in Berlin and Andreas Eiermann in Baden-Baden.
[67] saai, work archive Egon Eiermann, Eiermann House, Baden-Baden, files after 1970.
[66] The value had been estimated internally by the city at around two million marks.
[69] The masonry damage is currently still evident in the completely dilapidated plunge pool in the garden, which is filled with gravel, and in the walls of the laundry drying area cut into the slope to the east of the house. Both of these structural elements, which are important for the overall layout of the property, have not yet been restored in 2023.

Publications on the Eiermann House (selection)

Brigitte Eiermann, »Egon Eiermann, Haus und Nebenhaus in Baden-Baden«, *Architektur und Wohnform, Innendekoration*, 71st vol., 1963, no. 7, pp. 291–307.

»Einfamiliehus in Baden-Baden«, *Architekten*, 1964, no. 16, pp. 330 ff.

Guilia Veronei, Bruno Alfieri, *Lotus. Architectural annual 1964–1965*, Mailand 1964, pp. 206 ff.

»Una casa per ciascuno«, *L'architettura*, 10th vol., 1964, pp. 182 f.

Eberhard Schulz, »Das eigene Haus des Architekten«, *Frankfurter Allgemeine Zeitung*, 13.06.1964.

Eberhard Schulz, »Das eigene Haus des Architekten«. *Die Prediger mit dem Reißbrett*, Stuttgart 1964, pp. 31 ff.

Heinz W. Krewinkel, »Haus und Nebenhaus in Baden-Baden. Architekt: Prof. Egon Eiermann«, *Glasforum*, 1964, no. 2, pp. 4–9.

»Allemagne. Maison de l'architecte à Baden-Baden«, *Technique & Architecture*, 26th vol., 1965, no. 2, pp. 152 ff.

»Egon Eiermann. Das Detail ist das einzig Noble«, *Schöner Wohnen*, 1965, no. 7, pp. 58–65.

»Baden-Baden. An architect's home and guest house. Maison d'un architecte avec dépendance. Haus eines Architekten«, *ac, Revue internationale d'amiante-ciment. Internationale Asbestzement-Revue. International asbestos-cement review*, 43, 1966, no. 3, pp. 28–31.

H. O. Eckhardt, »Woonhuizen in Baden-Baden, architect: Prof. E. Eiermann«, *Bouw*, 1966, no. 26, pp. 1010/1011.

»Habitations à Baden-Baden. Egon Eiermann, architecte«, *L'Architecture d'Aujourd'hui*, 36th vol., 1966, no. 124, p. 63.

»Eiermann's Own«, *The Architectural Review*, 1966, no. 838, pp. 392 f.

»Architektenhaus in Baden-Baden«, in: Werner Weidert, *Einfamilienhäuser international*, Stuttgart 1967, pp. 68 ff.

Wend Fischer, *Geborgenheit und Freiheit. Vom Bauen mit Glas*, Krefeld 1970, pp. 300 ff.

»Haus Eiermann in Baden-Baden. 1960, 1961–62«, in: Wolfgang Pehnt, *Neue deutsche Architektur 3*, Stuttgart 1970, pp. 46 ff.

»Egon Eiermann, Eiermann House« in: Yukio Futagawa, *Global Interior 3. Houses in Northern Europe*, Tokio 1972, pp. 136 ff.

Wulf Schirmer (ed.), *Egon Eiermann 1904–1970. Bauten und Projekte*, Stuttgart 1984, pp. 186–189.

Lore Kelly, »Filigrane Leichtigkeit«. in: *Raum und Wohnen. Schweizer Magazin für Architektur, Wohnen und Design*, 1993, no. 2, pp. 38–48.

Lore Kelly, »Radikal modern«, in: *Wohndesign. Internationales Magazin für Architektur, Wohnen und Design*, 1993, no. 4, pp. 59–66.

Karin Kirsch, »Egon Eiermann, Wohnhaus und Atelier in Baden-Baden«, in: *Die neue Wohnung und das alte Japan. Architekten planen für sich selbst*, Stuttgart 1996, pp. 160–181.

Friedrich Grimm / Clemens Richarz, *Gestalten mit der Welle*, Stuttgart / Zurich 1998, pp. 32–37.

Günter Mader, »Ein Garten von Egon Eiermann«. in: *Gartenkunst des 20. Jahrhunderts. Garten und Landschaftsarchitektur in Deutschland*, Stuttgart 1999, pp. 138–141.

Clemens Kieser, »›Ich wollte kein Wohnhaus mehr bauen‹. Die Villenbauten Egon Eiermanns in Baden-Baden«, *Denkmalpflege in Baden-Württemberg, Nachrichtenblatt des Landesdenkmalamtes*, vol. 29, 2000, no. 4, pp. 254–260.

Brigitte Eiermann, »Wohnhaus Eiermann, Baden-Baden, Krippenhof«, in: *Egon Eiermann, Bauten in Baden-Württemberg 1946–1972*, ed. by the Egon-Eiermann-Gesellschaft e.V., n. p., 2000, pp. 92–99.

Peter Krebs, »Wohnhaus Eiermann, Egon Eiermann (1904–1970)«, *Baumeister*, 98th vol., 2001, no. 4, pp. 72–77.

Egon Eiermann (1904–1970). Zwei Wohnhäuser in Baden-Baden. Ein Stück Deutsche Architekturgeschichte, Bund Deutscher Architekten BDA, Kreisgruppe Baden-Baden, Rastatt, Ortenau, Baden-Baden 2002.

Clemens Kieser, »Wohnhaus Eiermann Baden-Baden, 1959–1962«, in: *Egon Eiermann 1904–1970. Die Kontinuität der Moderne*, exhibition catalogue, Städtische Galerie Karlsruhe, Bauhaus-Archiv, Berlin, 2004/2005, pp. 194–197.

Gennaro Postiglione (ed.), *Hundert Häuser für hundert europäische Architekten des zwanzigsten Jahrhunderts*, Cologne / London / Los Angeles / Madrid / Paris / Tokyo 2004, pp. 94–99.

Ulrich Coenen, newspaper articles on Egon Eiermann and his houses in Baden and the renovation of the Eiermann House, *Badisches Tagblatt*, Baden-Baden, 10.2.2021, 11.9.2021, 5.1.2022, 13.1.2022, 14.1.2022, 18.1.2022, 20.1.2022, 25.1.2022, 27.1.2022, 3.2.2022, 8.2.2022, 9.2.2022, 11.2.2022, 12.2.2022, 14.2.2022, 2.8.2023.
(The contnent of the articles will be published before the end of 2023 by the Mainz publishing house in Aachen as a publication entitled *Egon Eiermann in Mittelbaden – Anmerkungen zu seinen Villen in Baden-Baden und seinen Gewerbebauten in Offenburg*).

1. Blick von der tiefer gelegenen Straße auf die Hausgruppe, 2023. (Photo: Gerhard Kabierske.)
2. Die bergseitige Straße mit dem Zugang zum Haupthaus, 2020. (Photo: Martin Kunz.)
3. Blick auf den Hauseingang an der bergseitigen Straße, 2023. (Photo: Gerhard Kabierske.)

1. View from the lower road to the group of houses, 2020. (Photo: Martin Kunz.)
2. The uphill road with the access to the main building, 2020. (Photo: Martin Kunz.)
3. View of the the access to the main building on the uphill road, 2023. (Photo: Gerhard Kabierske.)

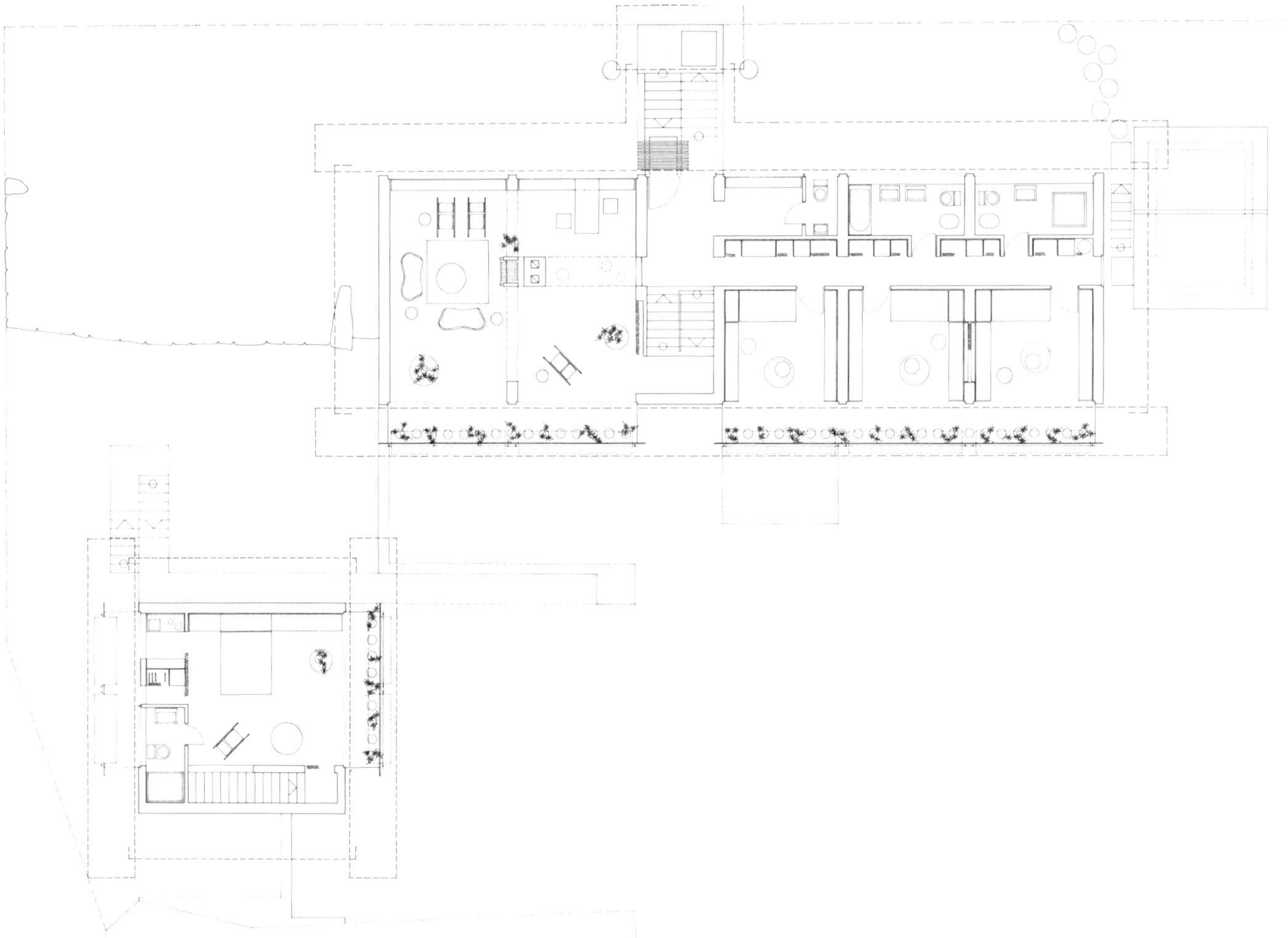

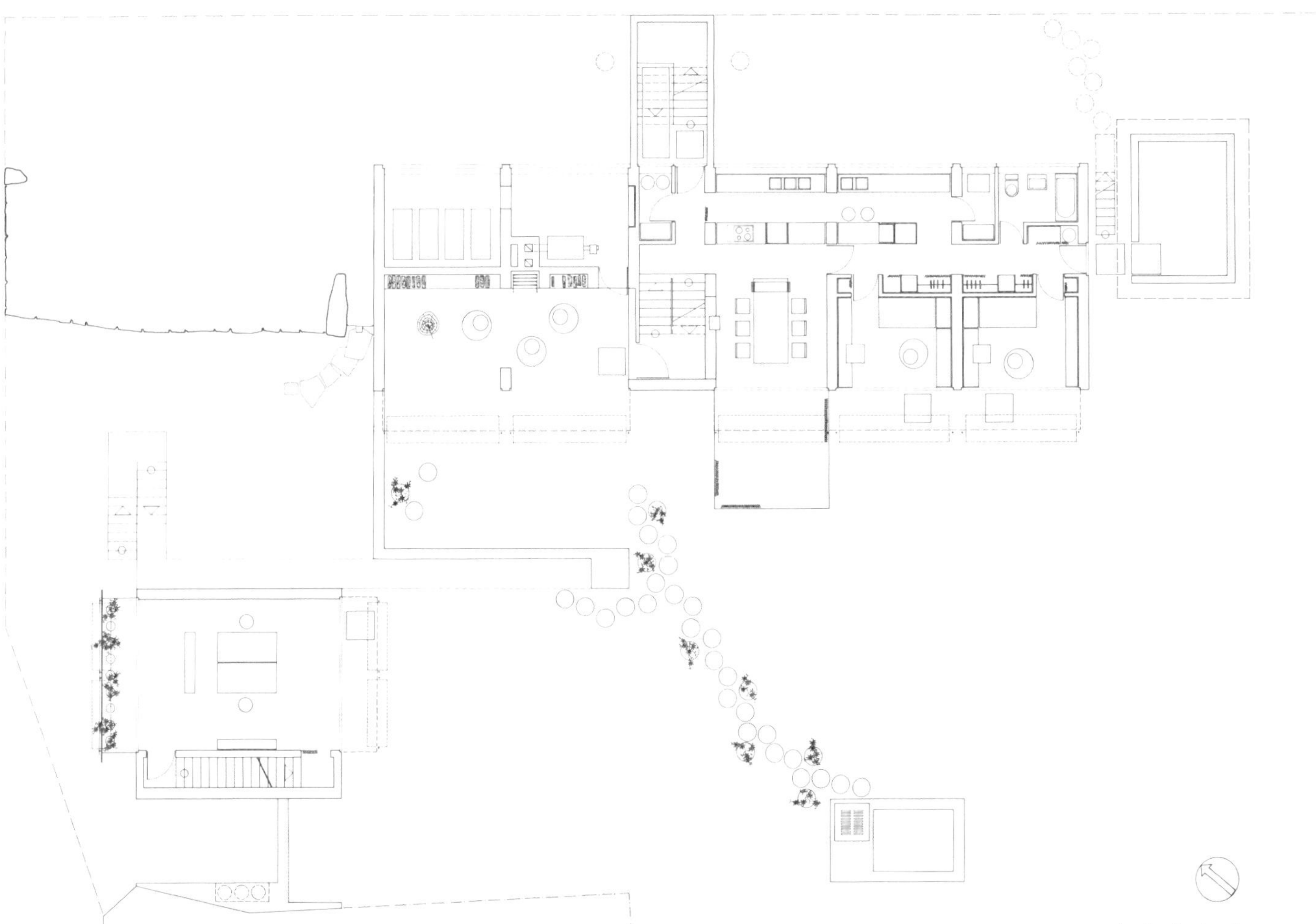

1. Grundrisse der oberen Geschosse von Haupthaus und separatem Atelierhaus. Im Haupthaus der Hauseingang mit Garderobe. Am Flur gereiht die Schlafräume sowie das Herren- und das Damenbad. Als Verbindungsglied der versetzten Geschosse das zentrale Treppenhaus. Eine halbe Treppe tiefer der Wohnraum mit frei stehendem Kamin. Im Atelierhaus das Wohnstudio mit eigener Erschließungstreppe.
2. Grundrisse der unteren Geschosse. Im Haupthaus zur Bergseite die Küche, zur Gartenseite der Eßraum mit vorgelagerter Terrasse, daneben die von der Schmalseite her erschlossene Einliegerwohnung. Unter dem Wohnraum die Heizung, davor zum Garten hin die offene Loggia mit offenem Kamin und Holzlager an der Rückwand. Im Atelierhaus der Arbeitsraum.
3. Schnitte durch Haupthaus (Schlafräume, Treppenhaus, Wohnraum) und Atelierhaus (Arbeits- und Wohnraum, Treppenhaus).
4. Ansichten (von Nordwesten, Südwesten, Nordosten, Südosten).

1. Floor plans of the upper floors of the main house and the separate studio building. In the main building, the entrance with cloakroom. The bedrooms and the men's and women's bathrooms are lined up along the corridor. The central staircase connects the staggered floors. Half a stairway down is the living room with a free-standing fireplace. In the studio building, the living studio with its own access staircase.
2. Floor plans of the lower floors. In the main building the kitchen on the mountain side, on the garden side the dining room with a terrace in front, next to it the gran-ny annex accessed from the narrow side. Under the living room the heating, in front of it towards the garden the open loggia with open fireplace and wood storage at the back wall. In the studio building the workroom.
3. Sections through the main building (bedrooms, staircase, living room) and the studio building (study, living room, staircase).
4. Views (from north-west, south-west, north-east, south-east).

Die folgenden Photographien von Horstheinz Neuendorff enstanden alle im Jahr 1963, kurz nach Fertigstellung des Gebäudes.

The following photographs by Horstheinz Neuendorff were all taken in 1963, shortly after completion of the building.

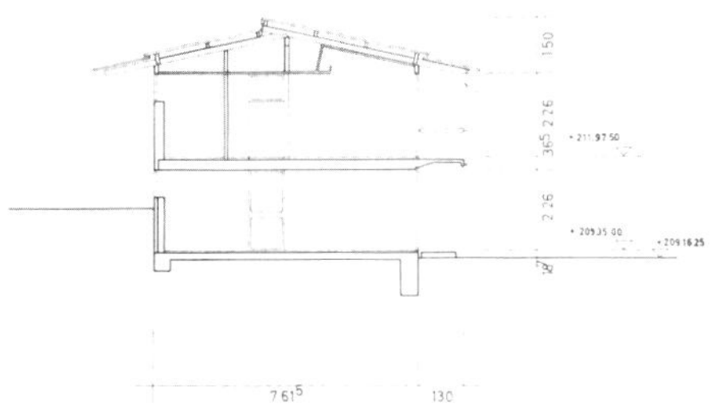

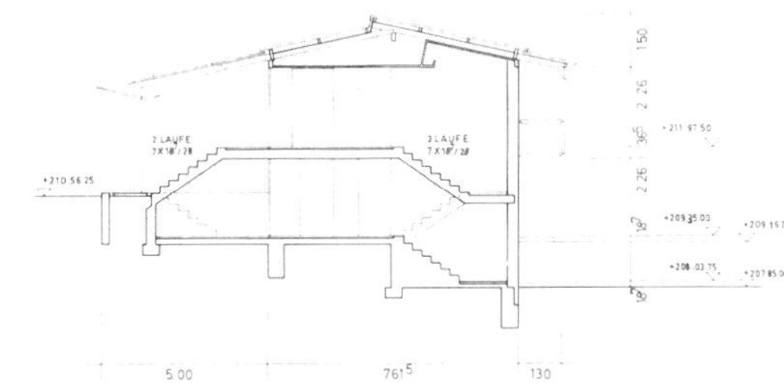

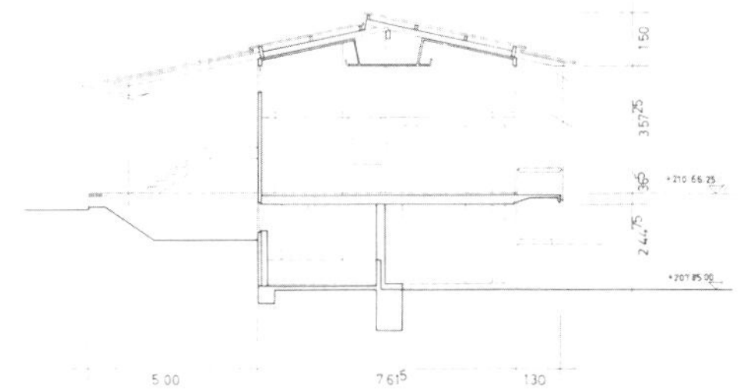

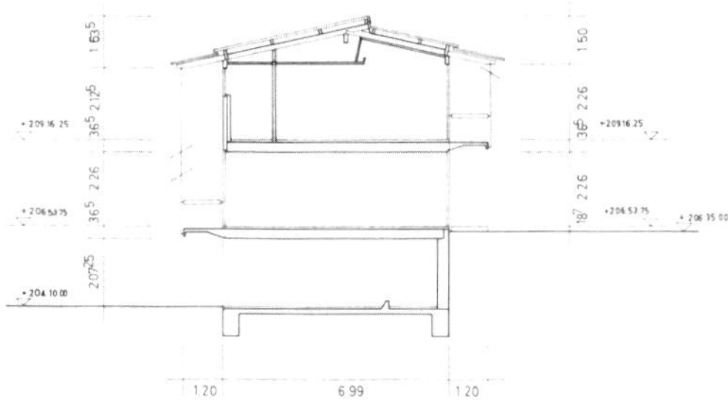

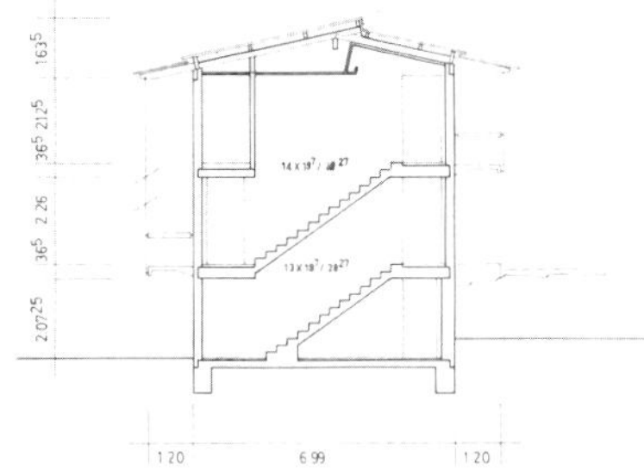

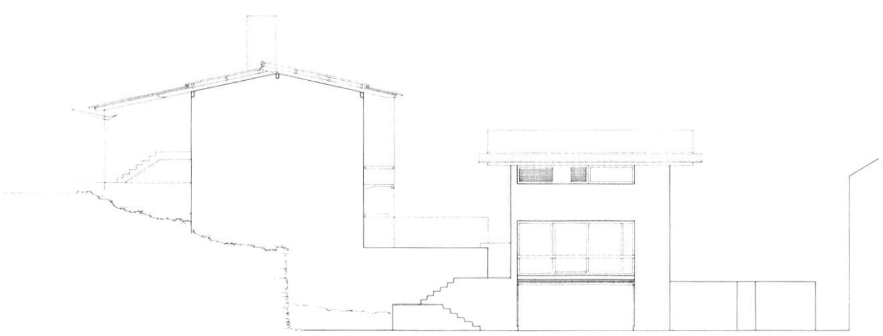

ANSICHT KRIPPENHOF NORD-WEST

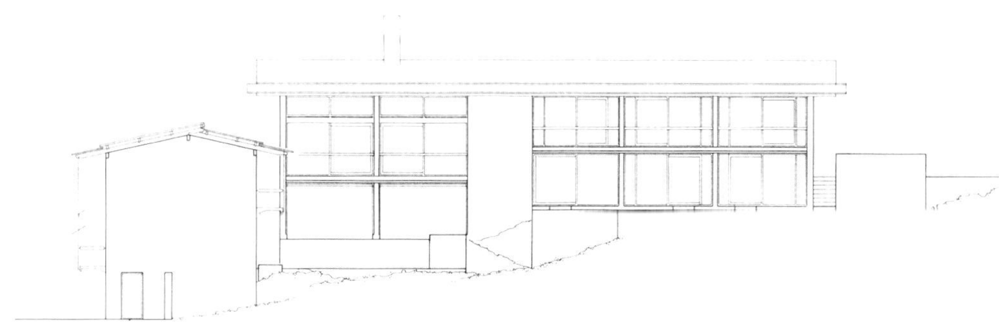

GARTENANSICHT SÜD-WEST

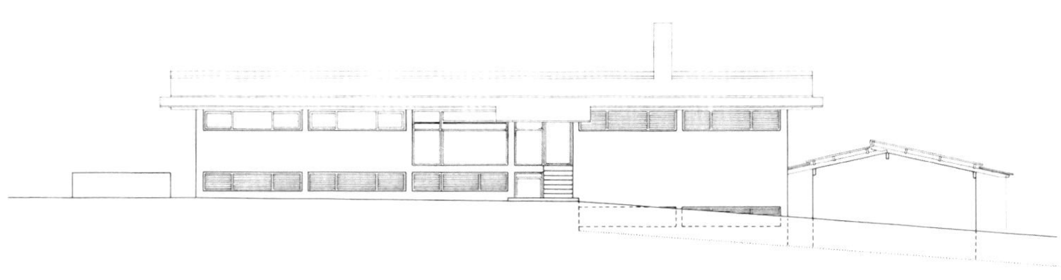

STRASSENANSICHT NORD-OST

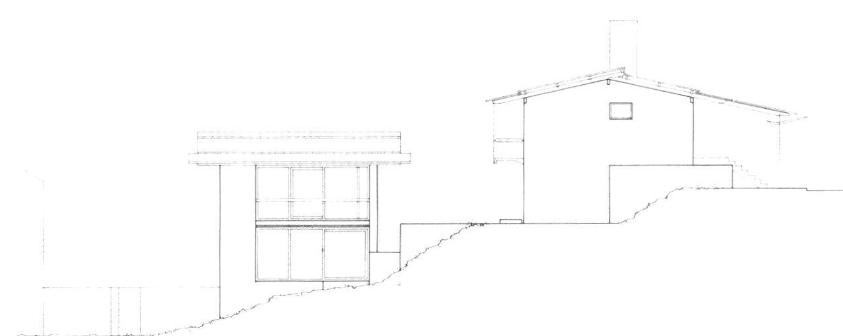

GARTENANSICHT SÜD-OSTEN

KA
HE 900

S. 46/47
5. Blick auf die Gebäudegruppe aus Haupt- und Atelierhaus mit Garage von Nordwesten. In der Mitte der bühnenartige Treppenaufgang zum Garten, links die in den Neubau einbezogene Böschungsmauer des früheren Krippenhofs.

pp. 46/47
5. View of the group of buildings consisting of main building and studio building with garage from the north-west. In the centre, the stage-like stairway to the garden, on the left the embankment wall of the former Krippenhof integrated in the new building.

S. 48/49
6. Nachtaufnahme von Nordwesten mit Beleuchtung durch Strahler mit frei verlaufenden Kabeln am Fassadengestänge. Der Zugang zur Garage besteht aus frei hängenden Holzstangen.

pp. 48/49
6. Night shot from the north-west with illumination by spotlights with freely running cables on the façade rods. The access to the garage consists of free-hanging wooden poles.

7. Blick auf das Haupthaus von Osten mit Zugang von der bergseitigen Straße. Am flach geneigten Giebel erkennbar das Rohr zur kühlenden Wasserberieselung der Dachfläche.
8. Blick auf das Haupthaus von Norden mit der Inszenierung des Eingangs bis hin zum Straßenrand.

7. View of the main building from the east with access from the up-hill side street. The pipe for the cooling water sprinkling of the roof surface is visible on the flat sloping gable.
8. View of the main building from the north with the staging of the entrance up to the roadside.

9. Blick auf den Hauseingang mit dem flach geneigten, abgestuften Faserzementdach.
10. Detailansicht des Hauseingangs mit Aufgang in das obere Geschoß und Abgang in das untere Geschoß.
11. Detailansicht des Hauszugangs mit den segelartigen Seitenwangen und weit überstehendem Vordach.

9. View of the entrance to the house with the shallowly pitched, stepped fibre-cement roof.
10. Detailed view of the house entrance with up stairs to the upper floor and down stairs to the lower floor.
11. Detailed view of the house entrance with the sail-like side cheeks and the projecting canopy.

S. 54/55
12. Blick auf die Gartenseite des Haupthauses mit der Terrasse vor der offenen Gartenloggia und dem höher gelegenen Eßraum von Südwesten, links das Atelierhaus. Auf dem gemauertem Sockel eine kapitellartig aufgestellte Baumwurzel, daneben die Trittstufen in den Garten sowie im Rasen Entwässerungsrinnen aus Kies. Im Vordergrund die Gartendusche am Wasserbecken.

pp. 54/55
12. View of the garden side of the main building with the terrace in front of the open garden loggia and the higher dining room from the south-west, the studio building on the left. On the brick plinth a tree root set up like a capital, next to it the stepping stones in the garden and drainage channels of gravel in the lawn. In the foreground, the garden shower at the water basin.

13. Blick von der Terrasse vor dem Eßraum zum Atelierhaus. Im Vordergrund die wie eine Skulptur aufgestellte Baumwurzel.
14. Gartenseite von Haupt- und Atelierhaus mit der von Vorhängen umfaßten Terrasse vor dem Eßraum.
15. Blick vom steil ansteigenden Garten auf das Haupt- und das Atelierhaus, links das Wasserbecken.

13. View from the terrace in front of the dining room to the studio building. In the foreground, the tree root set up like a sculpture.
14. The garden side of the main building and the studio building with the terrace in front of the dining room enclosed by curtains.
15. View of the main building and the studio building from the steeply rising garden, with the water basin on the left.

16. Nachtaufnahme des Haupthauses. Deutlich wird die Transparenz der Gartenfassade, oben die Schlafzimmer, unten die Terrasse vor dem Eßraum mit ihren Außenvorhängen.
17. Nachtaufnahme der Gartenseite des Atelierhauses, unten der Arbeitsraum, oben das Wohnstudio. Die Fußböden im Inneren sind mit runden Fliesen, der Außenbereich ist mit Kies belegt.

16. Night shot of the main building. The transparency of the garden façade becomes clear, above the bedrooms, below the terrace in front of the dining room with its exterior curtains.
17. Night shot of the garden side of the studio building, below the workroom, above the living studio. The floors inside are covered with round tiles, the outdoor area is gravelled.

S. 60, 61
18. Blick aus dem oberen Geschoß des Atelierhauses auf das Haupthaus mit der Terrasse vor der Gartenloggia und dem höher liegenden Terrasse vor dem Eßraum.
19. Blick vom oberen Geschoß vor den Schlafzimmern entlang der Gartenseite des Haupthauses zum tiefer liegenden Wohnraum.

pp. 60, 61
18. View from the upper floor of the studio building to the main building with the terrace in front of the garden loggia and the higher terrace in front of the dining room.
19. View from the upper floor in front of the bedrooms along the garden side of the main building to the lower lying living room.

20. Blick auf die Gartenfassade des Atelierhauses mit weit überstehendem Faserzementdach, den in die auskragende Bodenplatte des oberen Geschosses eingelassenen Blumentöpfen sowie dem Fassadengestänge mit dem segeltuchbespannten Sonnenschutz. Vor der Glasfront des unteren Geschosses eines der vergitterten Schiebeelemente, um Tiere bei geöffneter Glaswand vom Inneren fernzuhalten.
21. Blick aus dem oberen Geschoß des Atelierhauses auf den steil abfallenden Garten mit den zum Wasserbecken führenden runden Trittstufen sowie den gekiesten Entwässerungsläufen für das Regenwasser.

20. View of the garden façade of the studio building with its widely projecting fibre-cement roof, the flower pots embedded in the cantilevered floor slab of the upper storey and the façade frame with the canvas-covered sunshade. In front of the glass front of the lower storey, one of the barred sliding elements to keep animals out when the glass wall is open.
21. View from the upper floor of the studio building onto the steeply sloping garden with the round stepping stones leading to the water basin and the gravelled drainage channels for the rainwater.

22. Blick auf die Vorbildern aus Japan entlehnten Trittsteine und Pflanzkübel aus runden Betonrohrelementen.
23. Die Trittsteine führen hinunter zum Wasserbecken mit Holzrost für die Gartendusche, rechts angeschnitten die skulpturale Baumwurzel.

22. View of the stepping stones and planters, borrowed from Japanese examples, made of round concrete pipe elements.
23. The stepping stones lead down to the water basin with a wooden grate for the garden shower, the sculptural tree root cut in on the right.

24–26. Der Wohnraum im nordwestlichen Teil des Haupthauses mit dem frei stehenden offenen Kamin. Horizontale Träger unterteilen die größere Raumhöhe. Sie dienen zur Aufstellung von Grünpflanzen, die dem Raum den Eindruck eines Wintergartens verleihen. Der Boden besteht wie im ganzen Haus aus verschiedenfarbigen runden Keramikfliesen, die in Estrich verlegt sind und sich zu eingestreuten Blütenmotiven verdichten. Die Möblierung nach Entwürfen von Eiermann mit Ausnahme von zwei Thonet-Schaukelstühlen.

24–26. The living room in the north-western part of the main building with the free-standing open fireplace. Horizontal beams divide the greater room height. They serve to place green plants, which give the room the impression of a winter garden. The floor, like in the rest of the building, consists of variously coloured round ceramic tiles laid in floor pavement and condensed into interspersed flower motifs. The furniture is based on designs by Eiermann, with the exception of two Thonet rocking chairs.

27. Blick in die Küche im unteren Geschoß. Rechts hinter dem Herd die mit einer Jalousie geschlossene Durchreiche zum Eßraum.
28. Blick vom Eßraum durch die Jalousie in die Küche.
29. Blick vom Eßraum in den höher gelegenen Bereich von Treppenhaus und Wohnraum. In die Brüstungswand zwischen Eßraum und Treppenhaus eingelassen ein farblich kontrastierender Sockel zur Aufstellung einer Kleinplastik.

27. View of the kitchen on the lower floor. On the right behind the cooker, the hatch to the dining room is closed with blinds.
28. View from the dining room through the blinds into the kitchen.
29. View from the dining room to the higher area of the staircase and the living room. In the parapet wall between the dining room and the staircase, a colour-contrasting plinth for the installation of a small sculpture.

30–32. Die Schlafräume von Egon und Brigitte Eiermann im oberen Geschoß des Haupthauses. Die große Wandöffnung zwischen den beiden Räumen wird durch ein offenes Regal mit beidseitigen Arbeitsplatten verstellt. Mit einem mittig integrierten Vorhang lassen sich die Raumkompartimente zusätzlich trennen.

30–32. The bedrooms of Egon und Brigitte Eiermann on the upper floor of the main building. The large opening in the wall between the two rooms is closed by an open shelf with worktops on both sides. The room compartments can be additionally separated with a curtain integrated in the centre.

Haus Eiermann
Krippenhof 16–18
76530 Baden-Baden

Grundstücksgröße / Property size: 1.800 qm
Gesamtwohnfläche/Total floor space: 419 qm
Umbauter Raum/ Enclosed space: 1.719, 573 cbm

Planungszeit / Planning time: 1958–62
Bauzeit / Construction time: 1961/62

Bauherren / Client: Egon Eiermann, Brigitte Eiermann
Architekt / Architect: Egon Eiermann
Mitarbeiter Entwurf / Design staff: Rudolf Wiest, Abdullah Brechna, Kurt Huppert
Mitarbeiter Bauleitung / Construction management assistant: Kurt Huppert
Statik / Static: R. Lux, Karlsruhe
Prüfstatik / Static verification: Karl Winkelmann, Karlsruhe
Beratender Gartenarchitekt / Consulting garden architect: Toni Jelinek, Frankfurt am Main
Beteiligte Firmen (Auswahl) / Companies involved (selection): K. Bold KG, Bauunternehmen, Baden-Baden; Vereinigte Speyrer Ziegelwerke AG, Speyer; Alfons Strack, Zimmermeister, Baden-Baden; Gustav Müller, Stahlbauwerk, Offenburg; Metallbau Groke, Karlsruhe; Eternit AG, Heidelberg-Leimen; Johannes Haag, Heizung & Lüftung, Karlsruhe; Niederrheinische Baukeramik Gebr. Heimann, Vrasselt; Theo Naumann, Platten- und Fliesen, GmbH; Wilhelm Fricke, Malermeister, Kassel; Gretsch Unitas G.m.b.H., Baubeschläge, Stuttgart; L. Stromeyer & Söhne, Zeltfabrik, Konstanz; Seilwerk Dreher, Karlsruhe; Eduard Pfeifer, Hanf- und Drahtseile, Memmingen; Wilde & Spieth, Möbelfabrik, Esslingen; Markstahler & Barth, Möbelfabrik, Karlsruhe; Heinrich Neudeck, Beleuchtungskörper, Bruchsal

Sanierung der Terrassen / Renovation of the terraces: 2007/08
Bauherr /Client: Prof. Dr. Thomas Fischer
Architekten/ Architekten: langensteiner bienhaus architekten, Ettlingen, Ulrich Langensteiner

Gesamtsanierung / Overall renovation: 2020/21
Bauherren / Clients: Thomas Nitschke, Heiner Oppermann
Architekten / Architects: no w here architekten, Stuttgart, Karl Amann